Beyoncé

Tshepo Mokoena

Laurence King Publishing

For my mother and my sister

LAURENCE KING

First published in Great Britain in 2021
by Laurence King Publishing
an imprint of The Orion Publishing Group Ltd
Carmelite House, 50 Victoria Embankment
London EC4Y 0DZ

An Hachette UK Company

1 3 5 7 9 10 8 6 4 2

Design © 2021 Laurence King Publishing
Text © 2021 Tshepo Mokoena

A CIP catalogue record for this book is
available from the British Library.

ISBN 978 1 913947347

Origination by DL Imaging, UK
Printed in Italy by Printer Trento Srl

Cover illustrations by Bijou Karman

www.laurenceking.com
www.orionbooks.co.uk

CONTENTS

I. The Wallflower *5*

II. Girls Tyme *12*

III. Child of Destiny *25*

IV. Crossing Over *35*

V. 'I Know It's Gonna Be Great' *50*

VI. The Hustle and Hive *60*

VII. A Hard Year *71*

VIII. Through Her Eyes *80*

IX. Secrets, Surprises *89*

X. Beyoncé Inc. *99*

XI. Black Is Legacy *108*

XII. Being the Greatest *117*

Resources *122*

Index *125*

Acknowledgements & Picture Credits *128*

I.

The Wallflower

In a home video, shot in the back garden of her family's Houston residence, Beyoncé Knowles is on a mission. Not even the fuzz of early nineties VHS can obscure her magnetism. Aged eleven, wearing loose shorts and a sleeveless top, she rehearses a song alongside three other girls. They've arranged themselves in a horizontal line, weaving through closely choreographed moves across a wooden deck that looks like it might wedge a sharp splinter into an unsuspecting heel. A leg kicked up here; arms thrust out in angular symmetry there; alternating hands resting on shimmying hips – Beyoncé concentrates on every movement.

And it's no wonder: she and the fellow members of a singing, dancing and rapping group known then as Girls Tyme were two-stepping their way through a gruelling three-month rehearsal schedule. The band's first producer, Alonzo 'Lonnie' Jackson, had designed (and named) this rigorous 'bootcamp', smiling wryly even when he spoke about it years later. While other kids could drift through their summer holidays, as days stretched into each other in the humid, soaring heat, Girls Tyme was put to work.

Beyoncé's commitment to this strenuous programme set a standard she would follow for decades. She rose from this intensely focused childhood to a rarely experienced level of stardom. For that eleven-year-old child dancing diligently, there was no guarantee of fame, no certainty that a far-fetched hope could transform into a long-standing career. Yet Beyoncé managed to exceed everyone's expectations of success.

To grasp how a middle-class, Southern girl became a symbol to millions – of mainstream feminism, sexual confidence, traditional family values and creative influence – you need to trace the contours of her life story. In its overlooked corners hang the delicate strings tying together the essence of what has come to captivate the pop star's fans while simultaneously infuriating her detractors.

Beyoncé established her dominance in an industry that was never designed to empower an artist like her. As a young, Black woman, she made the most of being underestimated. As a woman, she navigated the traps set to both exploit and constrict her sexuality. As an artist determined to make sense of music as a business, she wielded her power to pursue work in film, apparel design and philanthropy. There is a fine line between a vanity project and a genuine passion for exploring another form of expression – Beyoncé has trodden it carefully, though not without missteps.

All told, her life serves as an exemplary study in just how much you can achieve when you're aware of your abilities *and* how to square the way that others perceive you with your vision of yourself. Beyoncé developed a tight grip on her image from a shockingly young age. That sense of control has informed her public persona ever since. Hers is a story that can be told from several viewpoints. But, as she has proven time and again, and will no doubt continue to, none matters more than her own.

* * * * *

On 4 September 1981, Beyoncé Giselle Knowles was born in Houston's Park Plaza Hospital, to Célestine 'Tina' Ann and Mathew Knowles. In what would later become Beyoncé fan folklore, Tina (now Tina Knowles-Lawson following her marriage to actor Richard Lawson in 2015) chose to name her daughter in homage to her own family. Worried that her name would die out, Tina named her daughter after an iteration of her New Orleans, Creole-rooted maiden name: Beyincé.

At the time, Tina's father warned her against the decision, finding it absurd that she would give a child a surname for a first name. Headstrong, Tina reminded her father that Beyincé was hardly a well-known name to anyone outside the family. In fact, her first-born child would be teased about it by her classmates. That it was a family surname made no difference to Beyoncé's peers. Her name simply marked her out, along with her lighter skin and looser curls, as different.

It's important to pause and consider what these differences would mean for a young Beyoncé. Within many Black communities around the world, and in the South in the US in particular, colourism establishes a hierarchy. Today, thanks to the centuries-old 'one drop rule', Black American identity straddles many appearances. It can encompass everything from melanin-rich skin tones and tightly coiled afro hair to looser hair textures, or brown eyes speckled with green. Just as European Americans might reel off the components of their lineage – 'a quarter Irish, half Italian' and so on – Black Americans can name their own diverse roots, whenever their ancestors' identities were successfully recorded.

Beyoncé's French-speaking Creole maternal grandparents could trace their origins back to Native American, white French, Spanish and African ancestry. As a result, Tina is categorized as 'redbone', or lightskin. And her children are thus lighter-skinned, too. Beyoncé's family would later mention how the singer's hair texture and skin colour seemed to invite negative attention from darker-skinned Black girls her own age. They wouldn't explicitly cite jealousy or even mention colourism by name, instead skirting around the issue. The end result? Beyoncé only really spent time with her family, be it at her mother's hair salon Headliners or in the Knowles home, the epicentre for rehearsal.

At first, Beyoncé showed no immediate signs of a future in the spotlight. Those who knew her in childhood have described a shy girl who struggled to build friendships with other children. In fact, her younger sister Solange (born in 1986, and now also a successful recording artist) has gone so far as to say Beyoncé 'never had friends'. For the first few years of her life, before she found the support of her bandmates in Girls Tyme, it wouldn't have been a stretch to describe Beyoncé as a loner.

This reserved child liked to dance, though. In the early 2000s, her parents told magazine *Texas Monthly* that Beyoncé had been the sort of child who would walk into a room and immediately try to make herself invisible, practically shrinking into the shadows. Her interest in dance gave them an idea: perhaps, with a gentle prod, she'd manage to make friends while taking part in an after-school dance class. Though they couldn't have known it then, this simple decision laid the groundwork for the rest of their daughter's life.

* * * * *

Some 18 years after dance teacher Darlette Johnson-Bailey happened to overhear one of her young students singing to herself, she prepared to stand before a live talk show audience. Beyoncé was, oddly enough, spending her 25th birthday appearing on *The Ellen DeGeneres Show*. And though the star didn't know it at first, her former teacher waited off-camera, as the show taped a special season-opening edition in Central Park, New York.

DeGeneres eased the conversation towards a surprise that she'd hinted at earlier. First, she cued up a couple of home videos of Beyoncé singing when she was about five or six years old. Then, DeGeneres asked who had first recognized her talent and Beyoncé recalled 'Miss Darlette', sweetly describing how much she owed to her. Finally: the reveal. DeGeneres shouted 'Come on out!' and Johnson-Bailey appeared onstage. After an emotional hug and presenting Beyoncé with a single pink rose, she told the delighted audience, 'I always knew she would be a star'.

As a 'plucked from obscurity' tale, it's hard to beat. After class one day, Beyoncé waited for her parents to pick her up while Johnson-Bailey cleaned up in the studio.

Johnson-Bailey was singing Lisa Stansfield's 'All Around the World' to herself – not particularly tunefully, in her view – and remembered her pupil joining in. 'Beyoncé finished the song for me. And she hit a note, and I said, "sing it again". Now, I remind you, she was a very shy girl.'

When Mathew and Tina arrived, Johnson-Bailey insisted to them that their daughter could sing. And by that, Johnson-Bailey meant the child could sing to a professional standard if given the training and support. Beyoncé's parents had never seen their daughter perform in front of an audience, although, of course, they knew she liked to sing to herself and around the house. They saw a different version of their daughter not long after, when Johnson-Bailey, with the family's permission, started to enter Beyoncé into talent competitions.

For her first performance, Beyoncé sang John Lennon's 'Imagine' at a talent show at the Catholic Montessori school she attended in Houston, St. Mary of the Purification. She was just seven and, according to her mother, competing against children as old as fifteen. Before the show, Mathew took his little girl aside to explain Lennon's lyrics. He called upon her knowledge of Martin Luther King Jr as a Black rights figurehead, casting the song's famous lines about living in peace and unity in a new light. Mathew pulled from within the song a kernel that he knew Beyoncé could interpret. Later in life, she would be able to do this on her own and often leaves hints and half-open doors in her lyrics for fans to decode. But first, she had to make it through her first-ever performance in front of an audience.

That day, Tina and Mathew watched their daughter become someone else – she was still Beyoncé, of course, but not as they'd ever seen her. The child who would slink quietly into a room seemed to shake off an outer layer, revealing the charismatic performer who had been hidden behind her social shyness. (With this transformation, Beyoncé showed the very first signs of the indomitable alter ego she would later christen 'Sasha Fierce'.) That day, the seven-year-old sang as best she could. And she won. Over the next couple of years, she entered talent shows and beauty pageants around the state and would grab the top spot in at least 30 more competitions.

This time was key to the development of the rest of her career. For the first time, Beyoncé's parents witnessed their daughter's talent, on a scale that stretched beyond the walls of their comfortable, six-bedroom home in Houston's middle-class Third Ward neighbourhood. When you consider how many children display singing talent but never pursue music as a profession, her ascent already stands out. Growing up in Houston could also have limited Beyoncé. Unlike families that decamp to one of the US's coastal cities for the sake of a talented child, homing in on the epicentre of the entertainment industries, the Knowles family stayed put.

Beyoncé continued competing, joining choirs while attending Parker Elementary Music Magnet school from 1990. But as her local profile grew, and a team of managers and producers started to form around her, one fact soon became clear. She would need a wider support structure. She would need bandmates.

II.

Girls Tyme

Not everything is as it seems. For Beyoncé to have hoisted herself up to the upper echelons of music fame, you might assume she grew up a well-connected showbiz kid. But in the late eighties, the entertainment industry was a foreign and vague idea to the singer – she was, after all, not yet a teenager. She knew she felt most alive when performing, a wallflower transformed into a centrepiece. But her forays onstage were largely limited to local competitions. You wanted to enter a pageant? Fair enough – they were openly looking for young talent. Beyoncé didn't need specialized power brokers to get her little foot in the door at this stage.

Her family were not connected to the music industry, either. Tina had briefly been a member of a girl group in her youth, but by this point, she was ploughing all her energy into her hairdressing business. Mathew Knowles worked in sales at the copier company Xerox. In interviews, Mathew tends to repeat that he spent these years engaged with 'corporate America'. He heralds it as the time in which he learned valuable lessons in how to later market his child and her friends as a product, to the biggest possible audience.

You could certainly say that what Beyoncé lacked in industry experience she more than made up for with drive.

When she began competing in pageants and shows, you could always find her mother by her side. Journalist J. Randy Taraborrelli notes in his extensive 2015 biography that it was Tina rather than Beyoncé's father who most supported their daughter's aspirations at this point. And true to Tina's devotion to the family unit – something that would prove crucial in later years when her first marriage began to atrophy – the attention she paid to Beyoncé tightened their natural bond.

Beyoncé arguably needed that support more than the average child. Between the ages of about six and nine, towards the end of the eighties, Beyoncé had already started to separate her performance experience from her school life. As had become clear during her first talent show, she could practically flip a performative switch, a light flickering from withdrawn to rambunctious. Of her time in beauty pageants and talent shows, she's said that once she found herself in front of an audience, she became 'a huge ham'. She continued: 'I don't know what came over me, but once I got my turn, I'd just strut my stuff and even finish by blowing a kiss to the crowd.' Watching recordings of her competitive childhood performances in her early twenties, Beyoncé joked that she was quite clearly doing too much. But, after a pause, came the kicker: it must have worked. She very often won.

In class, though, she was the voice rarely heard. As a former classmate of hers would later recount, they knew nothing about her involvement in beauty pageants. And at the same time, the girls she competed against could hardly implore her to share a word about school. When Beyoncé, speaking to the press, would later reflect on this time, she simply said: 'I was really serious, really focused: I loved to write music and I loved to sing.'

As she moved from solo talent shows and choirs to auditioning for her first group, Girls Tyme, Beyoncé started to reap the rewards of that 'really serious' nature. The formative years of the group, from about 1990 to 1993, included Beyoncé's first taste of recognition on a national level.

This period solidified her relationship with Kelly Rowland, first as a bandmate, then a friend, and then as someone she has referred to as a sister. 'I was really shy,' she has said. 'I loved being around my friends, which were the other group members. We were like sisters.' At face value, that reads as a touching statement; a sort of 'aww shucks' assessment of Girls Tyme's early years. But there's more to it. This closeness would gain importance in the face of media scrutiny at the peak of Destiny's Child's success.

The advent of Girls Tyme also hammered into Beyoncé the dogged work ethic that has come to define her career. Without these years, she would not have become a superstar. She certainly could have been signed by a record label. She easily could have recorded some promising demos before fading into the blur of similar R&B performers. The notion of Beyoncé as a cultural icon, though, can be traced back to her role as primary vocalist for the six-piece group Girls Tyme.

* * * * *

In the late eighties, two Houston women decided to change their lives. Deborah Laday and Denise Seals didn't have experience in the music business but set up joint company D&D Management with a simple mission. They were intent on creating a multi-part girl group, made up of singers, rappers, dancers and a 'hype master'. They felt it was about time some girls showed Kris Kross, New Edition and others that they also had what it takes. In particular, they wanted this group to feel more like a revue than any act currently gaining traction.

And so, their hunt began. In 1989, Laday and Seals put out ads and started scanning the stages at local performances. The pair auditioned Beyoncé and a host of other children, among them LaTavia Roberson, later a founding member of Destiny's Child. LaTavia's cousins, sisters Nikki and Nina Taylor, were recruited fundamentally as dancers within the revue set-up. With the addition of singers Jennifer Young and Staci Latoisen, dancer Christi Lewis and hype master Millicent Laday (Deborah's daughter), Girls Tyme and its parallel revue acts were set.

At that time, R&B vocal groups like En Vogue and SWV had justifiably fought their way into prominence. They did so not only for Black American listeners but later to a white mainstream, first in the US and then internationally. These acts were to set a new standard, picking up where the fifties and sixties Black girl groups had left off: to send shivers up a listener's spine with their harmonies and adapt to micro-trends in music, by switching from balladry to swaggering pop-funk wherever needed. Most importantly, groups like this were composed of line-ups so strong that any one member could sing lead, from track to track.

At the same time, acts from Boston's New Edition and Janet Jackson to newly formed trio TLC had proven an audience appetite for the tight, staccato beats of new jack swing. The genre extended an open arm between hip-hop and more traditional soul and R&B vocalizing – its rat-a-tat instrumentation leapt under smooth, harmony-rich vocals. Jimmy Jam and Terry Lewis still stand out as key producers of this sound. By the time Girls Tyme was taking shape, young Black listeners would have been introduced to the genre via Black music-oriented radio stations. But rap was still relatively niche for a white, mainstream audience in the early nineties – a factor that would shake Girls Tyme to its foundations.

Initially, though, the group had to learn to gel. Once the first line-up was finalized, Deborah Laday and Denise Seals quickly noticed that while the girls' talent ran deep, money was already tight. A sprawling group of this size would need frequent cash injections to facilitate recording sessions, costumes, rehearsals, travel to events and more.

According to the lore repeated in some interviews, Mathew Knowles managed Girls Tyme and then Destiny's Child. This narrative also appears in *Soul Survivors: The Official Autobiography of Destiny's Child* (2000), co-written with journalist James Patrick Herman. But the timeline involves more nuance than that approximation. Not long after the group came together, Laday turned to business-woman Andretta Tillman. Both women had worked together at Houston Lighting & Power and knew each other from the Yale Street Baptist Church.

The story of Tillman (who died in 1997) is often over-looked, but without her involvement, Beyoncé may never have found comfort and experience as part of a group. And beyond that, Mathew Knowles would never have become his daughter's manager – Tillman took him under her wing, according to her business partner at the time, Brian 'Kenny' Moore. In Moore's words, Tillman taught both himself and Knowles everything they'd need to know about the music industry.

Tillman had received a large sum of money through an insurance claim after her husband and baby daughter died in a 1986 car accident. Pat Felton, a friend of Tillman's, said that she started a group 'because of the death of her daughter'. According to Felton, Tillman told her that 'whatever it took for them to have voice lessons, modelling, how to speak', no expense would be spared. Tillman was actually Beyoncé's first manager.

And Tillman shook up the Girls Tyme line-up, streamlining it to make the band easier to sell to prospective record labels. A somewhat excitable gaggle of girls could get together and perform as a hobby, sure. But that group was not well suited to a future of contractual wrangling – nor was it the easiest product to market. And so Tillman planned to shave the group down to six singers who could also learn to dance, cutting the hype master, DJ and principal dancers. Original Girls Tyme members had to re-audition for their places, competing with a whole new swathe of giddy children.

Through these auditions (still all before her tenth birthday), Beyoncé met a young girl named Kelendria Rowland. It wouldn't be an exaggeration to say that they became inseparable. In one respect, this bond became the centre of Beyoncé's social life. It set a template she would follow for the rest of her youth: she would make few friends who didn't also happen to be work colleagues.

In another respect, this phase in the evolution of Girls Tyme also introduced the young Beyoncé to the cut-throat reality of music as a business. And that's because the young singer not only had to deal with the sudden loss of friends and bandmates – Laday's own daughter, for example, didn't make the harsh cut – but was also forced to wrestle with fresh competition in the form of newcomer Ashley Támar Davis. The two girls never stood at odds with each other or clashed explicitly. But in subtle ways adults would pit them against one another based on their vocal skill. And the ultimate lesson from all of this would come from the smarting sting of defeat, on a national stage.

* * * * *

An eleven-year-old Beyoncé would have never predicted televised talent show *Star Search* panning out the way it did. In autumn 1992, Tillman used the connections of two music producers to land what she believed would be the reduced Girls Tyme's big break. The first was Alonzo 'Lonnie' Jackson. As mentioned, he had developed the gruelling 'bootcamp' training regime for the girls, later overseen by Mathew Knowles. (In almost every interview with Destiny's Child, Knowles would be awarded sole credit for the bootcamp concept, but according to Kenny Moore, it is an accolade that he does not fully deserve.) Jackson had become an integral part of the team of producers, co-managers and other handlers working with the girls.

He also happened to know white producer Arne Frager, who, although not himself a long-term part of Beyoncé's retinue, led the girls to a slot on *Star Search*.

Their first attempt at nabbing a record deal in 1991 had failed. Thus *Star Search* represented a fast-track to a potentially huge audience. The show first aired between 1983 and 1995, charmingly hosted by Ed McMahon. Each week, amateur talents (known as 'challengers') would square up to their category's reigning winner (the 'champions'). Comedians, solo singers, child vocalists and groups were among about 250 hopefuls picked from approximately 10,000 entrants per year, all vying for a $100,000 prize. *Star Search* certainly wasn't the first televised talent search of its kind – please see 1948's *Original Amateur Hour*, initially a radio show. But *Star Search* still set the template for the *Pop Idols*, *The Voices*, and Whoever's *Got Talents* that would later skip and preen in its wake.

For a show centred on competition, though, *Star Search* developed a knack for missing real winners. A decent number of early 2000s pop and R&B stars started their careers swallowing the bitter pill of defeat in front of *Star Search's* studio audience and judging panel, including Britney Spears (junior vocalist 1992), Aaliyah (junior vocalist 1989), Christina Aguilera (junior vocalist 1990), Justin Timberlake (junior vocalist 1992 – introduced as 'Justin Randall'), Usher (male vocalist 1991), the Backstreet Boys (vocal group 1993) and even Pitbull (then known as Armando Pérez, male vocalist 1994).

In fairness to the *Star Search* judges, a handful of winners also grew into stars in their own right, even if often relegated to niche genres (most often seen with country acts) or jobbing performers pinging from Broadway to Vegas. Some fought their way back to relevance, as was the case for 1987 junior vocalist winner Alisan Porter, who blossomed into the 2016 winner of *The Voice*. Another, quite fabulously, grew up to be queer style symbol and performer Billy Porter (trophy: male vocalist 1992). But the majority of *Star Search* winners faded into the mundane ebb and flow of everyday existence, running a local music company or making lattes at a café. They experienced the sudden high of hot lights and prize money before disappearing altogether into the normality of a life away from the roar of an audience. A life cushioned by the soft dent in a sofa, the gentle familiarity of a long-term partner.

So the stakes were high. Neither losing, nor winning and then being evaded by fame, seemed an option for young Beyoncé. Here's how she and her bandmates thought their appearance would go: first, a giggly flight to Florida (have you ever tried to get multiple children to calm down on a plane?); then some final rehearsing before facing up to competitors near their age. Naturally, all would go well, and they would win in their category, staying on to defend their victorious position and ultimately skip right towards a record deal.

* * * * *

In its six-piece format, Girls Tyme hinged upon two strong lead vocalists – Beyoncé and Ashley Támar Davis – backed in sumptuous harmony by Kelly, LaTavia and sisters Nina and Nikki Taylor. Given how tirelessly they rehearsed, they had little reason to believe they wouldn't prevail. The group would pile into Tina's hair salon, performing for a captive audience of women trapped under hair steamers and dryers. Moore and Jackson looked on as the girls obsessively watched and rewatched Jackson 5 and Motown performances on VHS, making mental notes. But at first, though Beyoncé surged through rehearsals with drive, vocally she didn't sound as mature as Davis.

Producer Tony Moore (no relation to Kenny and known as Tony Mo) worked alongside Jackson in the early days of Girls Tyme, co-managing the group. He reflected on Davis's talent, in 2019's podcast *Making Beyoncé*. 'The singer with the big voice was really in back then – the powerhouse, the Whitney Houston type of vocalist,' Mo said. 'And so Ashley came up under that. She was just a fantastic singer. She always was a wailer, which meant she had a voice that could fill up a room. The strong voice,' he clarified, after warbling mid-sentence in what could vaguely be described as the style of a banshee on a rollercoaster.

As Davis remembered it, she was told from the start that she wouldn't be the only lead singer in Girls Tyme. 'I was like, "OK great" – if you needed me to sing a song, I sang a song. If you needed me to sing background, I sang background.' However, a recording trip to California, about a year before the girls headed to Florida in October 1992, flagged how easily the delicate balance between both leads could be upset.

On that trip, Arne Frager agreed to help the girls record a demo at Plant Studios in Sausalito, where he had worked for several years. Beyoncé and Davis were flown over, without their parents or bandmates. (As harsh as it sounds, only their voices mattered – multitracking their vocals pretty much obliterated the need to fly all six members out.) As the session progressed, Frager, Jackson, Tony Mo and co-managers Tillman and Moore watched Beyoncé eclipse Davis. She did so subtly, not in terms of volume but in technical acumen and what you can only really term 'soul'. In no time, Beyoncé was recording entire songs on her own while Davis watched on after fluffing unexpected rhythms and complicated transitions.

This detail matters because a rift between the group's various handlers over their song choice for *Star Search* may well have contributed to Girls Tyme's defeat. The power of Davis's vocals begged for a ballad. Something like 'Sunshine', their optimistic, cutesy stage favourite, seemed an obvious choice. And Davis had shown she could belt it beautifully, both live and during the group's 1991 recording session. Beyond that, many *Star Search* champions, often in the female vocalist category, had stormed to victory by captivating judges and audiences using torch songs. It would have been a tactical choice, too. But Beyoncé had shown a level of skill that the management team could no longer ignore.

An argument erupted. 'Andretta and I were saying, "let's do a slower ballad",' Moore recalled. 'But Mathew, Arne and Lonnie wanted to go for hip-hop.' Tillman and Moore urged the group to let Beyoncé and Davis both shine. 'We felt if they got a ballad,' Moore continued, 'and went up there – young kids singing quality, "Sunshine" or something – we'll kill 'em.' Instead, they landed on a track to showcase Beyoncé over anyone else. This was no doubt boosted by Mathew Knowles inserting himself further and further into Girls Tyme's management structure. His role as the father of the girl with the most stage presence granted him leverage. It was decided: Girls Tyme would perform 'Talking 'Bout My Baby'.

And that turned out to be the wrong choice. The song is just OK, with a meandering melody heavily reliant on harmonies (which weren't perfect on the night) and on Beyoncé leading. Raps performed by both LaTavia Roberson and Davis spliced up the song – an almost absurd configuration since Davis was never considered a rapper.

As Tina would later say, 'This is a hip-hop thing, and *Star Search* didn't even know what hip-hop was.' Jackson admitted he'd pushed Girls Tyme to perform 'a song I shouldn't have' as well. Rap in 1992 was decades away from lunging into the mainstream. But Beyoncé wasn't ready for the group's defeat, as they stood in their shiny, primary-colour shorts and T-shirt costumes and watched the judges return their score. A perfect four stars greeted the champions, thirty-something rock group Skeleton Crew. Then the judges bestowed three stars on 'the hip-hop rappin' Girls Tyme', as Ed McMahon had intoned. They were done.

Beyoncé held it together until they were off-camera. Then, she collapsed into her mother's arms, a puddle of tears. *Star Search* had felt like an appearance three years in the making. In all that time, Beyoncé had worked herself as hard as she thought possible. Whether in rehearsals, or in the studio, or studiously watching footage of the greats, she thought she and her friends would triumph. All those trophies stacked up in her family's home surely would have stood for something. Instead, this loss exploded the notion that Girls Tyme could have it all. For Beyoncé, it became her first foray into life being unfair. All of the work had not led to a win – and for a child, that is a tough lesson to learn.

There was further fallout. As word got out between the show's taping and its broadcast that the girls had lost, it blew more wind out of their sails. The whole point of *Star Search* had been to help them shop for a deal. Now, somehow, their appearance had the opposite effect, sending A&R and talent scouts scurrying away.

To move away from the stench of their defeat, Girls Tyme had to rebrand. Tillman and Mathew renamed the group as Somethin' Fresh. By early 1994, they'd cycled through several other names – The Dolls, Cliché, Destiny – in a push and pull between various handlers and producers. Ultimately, they would stagger over a few more obstacles before Beyoncé found herself leading the biggest R&B girl group fans had seen in years. It was time for Destiny's Child.

III.

Child of Destiny

With her hair pressed to a glossy sheen, lips lined and wearing a neutral expression, Beyoncé perched precariously on the edge of a hotel-room bed. She was waiting for her turn to speak. In one of many late nineties Destiny's Child press interviews, she sat slightly angled away from her bandmates. The young singer wasn't in a bad mood or turning away in anger. Instead, at this early stage in the band's career as a four-piece, LaTavia Roberson stood out as the leader. She sat in the middle of the bizarre 'on the bed' set-up, with LeToya Luckett on her left and Kelly Rowland on her right. When interviewer Terry Marshall asked the group to introduce themselves, one by one, LaTavia even referred to herself as the 'spokeswoman' who 'everyone calls the diva', with a giggle.

Beyoncé, meanwhile, cast her eyes low towards the zany, patterned duvet cover or up to Marshall's face, off-camera. Marshall then grasped onto Beyoncé's star sign (Virgo) as the basis for a question. He positioned her as a mother hen, asking if she felt it was her role as a perfectionist to keep the group in line. Graciously, she smiled, agreeing. 'Whenever something needs to be done,' she said, turning towards the rest of the group, 'I'm the one to say: "Come on, y'all – we've gotta do this."'

On that day, this felt almost like an admission of a boring sternness. You could have sat through the brief conversation and thought Beyoncé was a bit of a joyless organizer. Few would have known the real significance of her words until years later. Indeed, Marshall approached the young women with all the quiet confidence of someone who had no idea he was speaking to a future superstar. He wasn't rude by any means but asked questions that implied Destiny's Child needed to prove themselves. Beyoncé already knew that would be her main challenge: staking out her claim. She may still have only been a teenager, but given the whiplash that had snapped her from opportunity to disappointment and back again since she was about eleven, she knew the group had to work.

By the dawn of the twenty-first century, the dynamic at play during that interview would change forever. Beyoncé would soon occupy the space at the centre of Destiny's Child, drawing audience eyes to her first and picking up the most behind-the-scenes experience as a producer and songwriter. Just as any teenager begins to blossom into who they are, the beginning of Destiny's Child crystallized Beyoncé's vision of herself.

To be clear, those first years in Destiny's Child weren't without internal turbulence. They certainly weren't free of public controversy. From line-up changes to Beyoncé's emergence as the only lead vocalist, several shockwaves threatened the young singer's smooth ascent to superstardom. Nonetheless, by 2002 Beyoncé had clarified her own sense of self. These years saw her start to differentiate between Beyoncé Knowles the person and Beyoncé the public persona. They clarified her instinct for image-making and damage control. A name incorporating the word Destiny implies a sense of conviction, a preordained certainty sent into the future like burning light flung from a star. Over time Beyoncé came to invoke it, using a deep-seated belief to drive her forward. Yet she knew there were no guarantees for Destiny's Child, and she would leave nothing to chance.

* * * * *

Entering her mid-teens, Beyoncé's hunger for the steady validation of a record deal continued to propel her forwards. The problems kept cascading, and she pushed through them, led by her father. Ashley Támar Davis had left the group in early 1993 and was swiftly replaced by Beyoncé's classmate, bubbly soprano LeToya Luckett. So the band name and personnel changes after *Star Search* were one thing, of course. But their failure to sign on the dotted line at a record label was another. And it wasn't for want of trying.

Between 1991 and the summer of 1993, Beyoncé and her bandmates were put through what are known as production deals no less than three times. Those deals entailed linking the group up with a producer who would record a demo and then try to shop said demo around at various labels. At the end of each production deal glowed the promise of a recording contract with a major label. Finally, a deal turned into more than a fleeting opportunity. After briefly moving to Atlanta, Georgia to record with producer Daryl Simmons, Beyoncé and her friends were signed by Elektra Records in a joint venture with Simmons's company. They'd made it!

Sadly, the elation wouldn't last. Beyoncé said that the first deal lasted about eight months 'and just as soon as we started recording, it fell apart'. The group stagnated without what they considered adequate support. 'Even at that age,' Kelly remembered, 'we could tell that we were not considered a high priority.' Their instincts were right: after a few months, the girls were dropped. 'When Kelly, LaTavia, LeToya and I read the letter from the president of the company confirming that we got dropped,' Beyoncé later said, 'all we could do was cry.'

Little is said about how Beyoncé was dropped, but that doesn't mean she hasn't acknowledged it directly. She wrote honestly about the experience in the Destiny's Child auto-biography *Soul Survivors* (2002). The overall media focus on the *Star Search* defeat rather than this moment skips over a few important details.

In order to get signed in the first place, Beyoncé had pushed herself and her bandmates. Hard. She wrote breezily about the diet she went on as an adolescent, to shake off her perception of being 'chunky'. As she put it: 'It's a shame that a kid would have to worry about her weight, but I was trying to get a record deal and that was a reality.' Lonnie Jackson's foundation for training the girls both physically and musically was formalized into the 'bootcamp' since referenced in many a press interview. And crucially, Beyoncé stepped into a keener awareness of how she was seen by other people. Part of bootcamp involved watching back tapes of the group's rehearsals. Beyoncé learned to pick up on, and pick apart, what she deemed her performance flaws.

This isn't unusual, of course – there's a reason dancers practise in front of floor-to-ceiling mirrors. There's another reason sportspeople watch back gameplay on repeat. What better way to digest the flow of a game and assess both their own and their opponent's weaknesses? Beyoncé applied this to her work as an artist, even as an adolescent and teenager. As such, when the group were finally signed to Sony/Columbia in 1995, after grabbing the attention of A&R scout Teresa LaBarbera Whites, the pressure was on. Throughout Destiny's Child's early years, Beyoncé carried the lessons of that rigorous time spent regrouping, between *Star Search* and the Elektra deal. She would need that fortitude to weather turmoil within the group, and in response to a scandal-hungry press. As LaTavia's 'spokeswoman' role diminished, Beyoncé became the face of not only Destiny's Child's successes but also of its conflicts. Luckily, she already had gained enough industry experience to ride out the storm.

* * * * *

At the beginning of their contract with Sony/Columbia, Destiny's Child thrived. Each of the group's four talented and beautiful young members was styled and media-trained to appeal to a slightly different type of fan. Famously, Tina insisted they each dye their hair a distinctive colour – blonde for Beyoncé, red for LaTavia, black for LeToya and blue for Kelly – so no potential fan would feel left out. In a group of four girls, each fan would ideally have at least one group member to idolize. But beyond a sellable look, they had the vocal chops too. Their self-titled debut album peaked at number 67 on the Billboard 200 chart, following its February 1998 release. And it brimmed over with breathy, punchy and catchy songs. During this moment in pop and R&B, few groups managed to hover in that sweet spot spanning both huge commercial success and raw vocal talent. The likes of SWV and En Vogue earned their stripes in Black music charts in the US, and elsewhere with key singles. But in terms of album sales, Destiny's Child established that they could handle both.

Soon, they were touring the US, opening for R&B all-male vocal titans Boyz II Men. Then, TLC sought Destiny's Child as world-tour support, which saw Beyoncé and her bandmates shimmying and harmonizing to a growing horde of fans. It seemed nothing could stop them. Until it turned out that paperwork might. In a bid to renegotiate their management contracts with Mathew Knowles (separate from their overall deal with Sony/Columbia) in late 1999, LaTavia and LeToya inadvertently relinquished their places in the group.

There are still elements of this story only known to the members of Destiny's Child, their lawyers and Mathew Knowles. But the ultimate result of the management dispute saw LaTavia and LeToya ejected from the group, in a way they described as completely unexpected. 'It was conflicts that were going on,' LeToya said at the time. 'But the departure was' – and she clicked her fingers – 'like this'. LaTavia described it as happening 'at the drop of a hat'.

From Beyoncé's perspective, what she heard of her bandmates' unhappiness with her father sounded like yet another attempt to derail the group. 'We always tried to work out our differences, we always tried to communicate. But we were having problems for a while now,' she said. A scramble followed. Publicly, fans wouldn't have had a clue about the battle. Not until two new group members struck poses on the beat, flipping their hair in colour-coordinated outfits for the video for new single 'Say My Name'.

Michelle Williams and Farrah Franklin seemed to appear from nowhere. To outsiders it looked like an audacious move, replacing group members as you would actors playing the same character in a soap opera. Ultimately, Farrah would only spend eight months in the group, with Destiny's Child settling on a trio formation.

Of course, by 2000, this sort of change had become the norm for Beyoncé. Since she was ten years old, she had seen that band members come and go to best serve the manager's vision or the group's progress. In this respect, she was particularly unlike people her age, exposed to the inner workings of a cut-and-dry industry. As the bandleader, Beyoncé risked becoming a punchline rather than a role model. Since her father was known to be the group's manager, the weight of press scrutiny dropped more intensely on her shoulders, heavy and sudden. TV and radio pundits gleefully tore into the group, mocking their member change tactic.

Around this time, in 2000, you would see some of the last interviews in which Beyoncé sits visibly annoyed. She never went as far as rolling her eyes, but speaking to the E! Entertainment channel or MTV News, Beyoncé deftly deployed a steely, straight-faced demeanour when asked about the then-infamous line-up change. While

Kelly Rowland openly spoke words caustic with sarcasm, matched with a smile, Beyoncé appeared quietly fiery. She insisted the wellbeing of the group was always her priority, and that bidding LaTavia and LeToya farewell represented losing all the 'bad seeds', in one interview. In another, she suggested Farrah (then eighteen years old) wasn't willing to sacrifice enough to commit to the group. Privately, LaTavia's departure did hurt Beyoncé. According to her mother, Tina, Beyoncé disappeared into her bedroom for days afterwards, slipping into what Tina characterized as depression. 'I stayed in my room for a week,' Beyoncé said. 'I couldn't talk.' When she returned to the public eye, she seemed to have steeled herself against the onslaught of what she and Kelly would simply term 'drama'.

But let's not linger on the largely private details of who felt wronged by whom. (LaTavia and LeToya sued Beyoncé, Kelly and Mathew, and the matter was settled in 2002.) Rather, this moment is crucial in illustrating Beyoncé's capacity to dig deep and steady herself through a potentially career-destroying shudder of public turbulence.

* * * * *

In the late nineties and early 2000s, young Black women in pop music were granted even less autonomy than they are today. Beyoncé was growing up in public, sharing a sliver of herself with the press and perhaps more with fans. But she could have been seen as just one in an interchangeable cohort of young women R&B artists whose purpose in the business was to titillate, generate revenue and do as they were told.

She took a risk, then, in being willing to front a group that changed 50 per cent of its line-up overnight. And she steamrolled through the change, rushing to teach Farrah and Michelle the 'Say My Name' choreography (an effort that failed – the group strike and hold poses in the video because the new members just couldn't learn the original routine). Beyond that, she confronted questions about the changes head-on. Establishing a career naturally meant accepting piles of press requests. And from print to broadcast, Beyoncé – with Kelly by her side – described their side of the story over and over again. When fans in the 2020s watch these clips back on YouTube, most comment that they 'miss this Bey' or 'miss when she used to talk'. And that's because her openness at this point translated into showing she had nothing to hide.

You could interpret her frankness as exasperation or frustration, a woman barely out of her teens having to bear the brunt of prying questions and *Saturday Night Live* sketches at her expense. But you can also see her public appearances at this time in another way. They look more like someone desperate to get on with their work. Every moment spent rehashing the shocking story of a new Destiny's Child was a moment diverted from rehearsing, scribbling lyrics, learning how to produce vocals in the studio. Say what you like about how ridiculous it may have been to adopt a Supremes-like group change in the nineties, but Beyoncé always had the talent to back up her actions.

The group were often either criticized or objectified for being 'too sexy' for their age. Some of their lyrics were considered too grown-up, particularly on *Destiny's Child* and second album *The Writing's on the Wall*. But these were foundational years for Beyoncé to perfect her craft as a musician. It's strange to think about now, but while Beyoncé seemed to court controversy, she was quietly getting to understand her own instrument – her belting, powerful voice – and available tools. Since that first recording session, when she upstaged Girls Tyme member Ashley Támar Davis aged ten, she hadn't stopped learning. In the studio, it became clear that she had a role to play on both sides of the soundproof glass. Her voice filled her head, layers upon layers of her developing tone delivering the right level of emotion on Girls Tyme tracks such as 'Blue Velvet' or '632-5792'.

So she carried those lessons with her, writing songs in her bedroom as a teenager while Girls Tyme and then Destiny's Child attempted to secure a record deal. Much is made of how Beyoncé is often credited as a songwriter alongside several other collaborators in adulthood. These comments usually seem to diminish her work as an artist, implying that unlike a 'real' musician, she can't sit down at a piano or guitar and write a song on her own.

But since childhood, she has filled notebooks with the sketches of choruses, hooks and lines that would later blossom into complete songs. You can return to the liner notes on Destiny's Child's early albums and find her name listed in credits beyond 'just' singing. As she matured into early adulthood, Beyoncé used her songwriting to push Destiny's Child ahead of their peers. She shaped the band's voice in music. And their fans – particularly women – were ready to listen.

IV.

Crossing Over

Beyoncé was just sixteen years old when Columbia released Destiny's Child's eponymous debut album in 1998. By then, on and off for six years, she'd entered recording booths, slid on clunky headphones and sung words written by someone else. Hours of practice had stretched the bounds of her abilities, her voice expanding like molten toffee. You could imagine it strung and swaying between soaring vibrato, breathy sighs, a growl accompanying skittering, rap-like verses. Vocally, by her mid-teens, she had shown herself more than capable of fronting one of the most exciting pop prospects coming out of the US. But she knew there was more. Plenty of young stars bring to life stories crafted by producers and songwriters. And certainly, that is not a choice to be denigrated. The music industry machine runs on collaboration, though it is prone to exploiting the most naïve in the room.

Instead, at this pivotal life stage, Beyoncé used her songwriting to establish Destiny's Child as pop music's ambassadors of self-assured empowerment. She moved smoothly from the generalist ballads and love songs of debut *Destiny's Child* to music with a message. And it only took a couple of years. By 2003, she had invented entire slang terms, some of which took on second lives outside the group's music. Most importantly for young female fans, the band's brand of feminism was presented as words of advice from a savvy, older sister. Warnings about layabout boyfriends quick to spend your money rather than their own ran deeper than the charts they topped. Ultimately, Beyoncé provided affirmations for young women who didn't yet have the vocabulary to tell their male partners they deserved better than they were getting.

Cynics may cry foul, seeing this shift towards feminism-lite as a purely commercial move. In fact, you can trace the roots of Beyoncé's inspirational songwriting for Destiny's Child back to her family. Between her financially independent mother and headstrong – sometimes to his own and others' detriment – father, Beyoncé picked up a certain amount of knowledge just by watching them live their lives. Their commitment to the church, for example, laid the foundation for Beyoncé's offstage philanthropy.

But what they left *unsaid* taught her just as much about how to move through the world. Beyoncé was still several years away from using visuals and song to highlight her Blackness and her pro-Black upbringing. But you can almost consider Destiny's Child's growth as a testing ground. Here, she saw how you could sing about complex social issues – financial freedom, respect in relationships, navigating controlling male partners – within the parameters of pop. You could do so and win awards. Sure, you might annoy a few people along the way. But she and her bandmates could handle that. Crucially, Beyoncé saw that she could set herself apart – and still win.

* * * * *

By early 2001 the entitled male tantrums had begun. Some listeners took issue with Destiny's Child, specifically with the group calling out sexism deeply rooted in so much of the behaviour casually exhibited by straight men. The album *Destiny's Child* had bobbed smoothly along, filled with love songs steeped in a hybrid R&B and neo-soul sensibility. Beyoncé helped the band mature on their follow-up album, released in 1999. She was beginning to take her first tentative steps over the bridge between adolescence and adulthood. And, when she channelled that into a change in the girls' sound, *The Writing's on the Wall* staked out new territory for the group.

Some of that derived from a certain sophistication found in the production, sure. Vocal harmonies rippled on songs such as 'Hey Ladies' and the huge single 'Say My Name'. Meanwhile, beats pieced together by rap heavyweights Missy Elliott and Timbaland, as well as Rodney Jerkins and Daryl Simmons (who had helped the group secure their Sony record deal), elevated the group towards a tighter, upbeat sound. Yet the lyrics caused a major stir. Once the drama of the group's line-up change had died down, following the release of the 'Say My Name' music video, listeners fixated on just what Destiny's Child was trying to say. The type of empowerment Beyoncé would develop into a calling card was rubbing men with traditional views (and, to be honest, non-feminist women) up in every wrong way possible. As a *Vibe* magazine cover story interview put it in February 2001, *The Writing's on the Wall* 'earned the group reputations for being everything from male-bashing gold diggers – a charge the girls heatedly deny – to new-millennium feminists out to challenge the bitches-ain't-shit posturing that plagued much of late nineties R&B and hip hop'.

This misreading of the group as bitter men-haters, stoking up conflict within otherwise happy straight couples, took time to undo. While promoting *The Writing's on the Wall*, Beyoncé and at points LaTavia had to defend their stance in interviews. During this era in pop music, women singers of their age were expected to be largely ogled and not heard. And you could tell their more forthright songs rattled male interviewers in particular. 'The song is not talking about all guys,' Beyoncé said of Billboard Hot 100 chart-topper 'Bills, Bills, Bills', during a 1998 BET (Black Entertainment Television) interview. 'A lot of guys are taking the song to heart, like "OK, they're calling all guys trifling". That's not what we're doing.' She underlined that the single was not commanding men to pay for everything. Instead – as the lyrics made clear if anyone was listening to the verses and not just the chorus hook – Destiny's Child was describing a specific scenario. In it, a boyfriend started off paying his way, then slipped towards spending more of his girlfriend's money. 'The girl is basically telling the guy to pay back the bills that he has run up.'

Simple? Well, it ought to have been. The pop-culture discourse around gender in the late nineties and early 2000s was still predicated on a dynamic built by (and for) straight men. For all the academic analysis and powerful, if incremental, change made by second- and third-wave feminists in the late twentieth century, patriarchy dug in its heels, refusing to budge. And as a result, any attempt made to drag into the light an imbalanced system that assumed female inferiority met with fierce resistance.

This extended, of course, to music. After all, why else would Beyoncé have to spend a substantial amount of time during an interview explaining a song, to placate male listeners and make its message seem more gentle? Her clarification that the song was not about 'all guys' reads now like a prototype of the #notallmen hashtag, the rebuttal slung out on social media any time a woman points out how patriarchy works as a system. Usually, offended men deflect and try to turn the systemic back into the personal. 'We don't all do this awful thing!' they cry, as though that dissipates the incessant crush of gender oppression.

In that BET interview, host Lorenzo Thomas baited Destiny's Child by engaging in whataboutery. He countered Beyoncé's description of 'Bills, Bills, Bills' with the notion that women 'have been doing that to men for eons'. By deflecting the issue, he also changed the subject of the interview and turned it back into an interrogation of women, of what they've been able to 'get away with'. Lorenzo seemed more concerned with dismissing Beyoncé's viewpoint rather than truly listening and responding to it.

* * * * *

Beyoncé didn't co-write songs such as 'Bills, Bills, Bills', 'Bug a Boo' and later 'Independent Women Part 1' in a vacuum. In 1999, a straight-talking jolt shuddered through pop-R&B songwriting, led by Black women. First came TLC's 'No Scrubs', released in February 1999. Its message to women insisted they had every right to ignore deadbeat, posturing men who hollered rudely for their attention. The song quickly became a dancefloor anthem, and a niggling thorn in the side of disgruntled men. It ended the year just outside the 20 top-selling songs in the US, according to *Billboard* magazine, shifting more than 800,000 units. 'Bills, Bills, Bills', released in June 1999, was even more commercially successful, selling at least 900,000 units. But both songs are united by more than a respectable impact on the charts. They embodied a certain demand for higher standards because they were co-written by the same woman: songwriter, former Xscape group member and television personality Kandi Burruss.

Thinking back to songs she was writing in the late nineties and early 2000s, Burruss summed that time up succinctly: 'a lot of people called it the male-bashing era'. She said she hates that term now, though it truly was wielded as a weapon to snuff out that brief, feminist spark in hugely popular music. Burruss and her 'No Scrubs' co-songwriter, former Xscape bandmate Tameka 'Tiny' Harris, always clarified that the song was about a very specific time in Burruss's life. 'My songs were a reflection of relationships that were going on, or that I had in that past life,' Burruss said, laughing. She considered her lyrics 'kind of like a diary' where she was inspired by what was happening at the time. Speaking to *Rolling Stone* in 2014, Tiny confirmed this. The song 'came from a previous relationship that [Burruss] was in,' she said. 'And we took that and wrote about what we call a scrub.' Together with Kevin 'She'kspere' Briggs, one of several producers drafted to work on *The Writing's on the Wall*, Burruss in particular developed a signature sound. A year later, she was also behind Pink's debut single 'There You Go', a hit about leaving behind a no-good, lying boyfriend after being wronged one too many times. A lilting harpsichord line ran through the song, similar to that which trilled on both 'Bills, Bills, Bills' and 'No Scrubs'.

Beyond sonics, though, these songs represented a wider moment. They told the personal stories of Black women, a torch picked up from the flame lit decades earlier by icons such as Bessie Smith, Dinah Washington, Aretha Franklin and Nina Simone. Put bluntly, Black women songwriters brought their often untold sides of the story into the charts in a no-holds-barred fashion, which stunned critics while delighting fans.

In full-on, sweetly bubblegum pop, the overriding message was more 'let me be who or what you desire', rather than 'if you can't do right by me, I'm gone'. Artists such as Britney Spears and Christina Aguilera – also just teens at the start of their careers – channelled the intensity of young love into music that pined with heartache and devotion. When major labels then brought Mandy Moore and Jessica Simpson into the market, to capitalize on the momentum created by Spears and Aguilera, they also followed suit. But Beyoncé's work, as both leader and songwriter in Destiny's Child, showed young fans another path. She proved that they could look for love while setting out the boundaries that a potential partner ought to think twice before crossing. Following in TLC's footsteps, she and her bandmates helped foster the environment into which singer Kelis would howl with rage on 'Caught Out There' in September 1999, and rapper Missy Elliott would release kiss-off track 'All N My Grill' in the same year.

In her personal life too, Beyoncé was far from a 'man-hater'. In early 2001, she ended a long relationship with childhood boyfriend Lyndall Locke – they had dated since she was twelve. About a year earlier, Jay-Z had contacted her for the first time after she recorded vocals for an act signed to both Sony/Columbia (her label) and Roc-A-Fella Records (his label). They bumped into each other again in October 2001, exchanged numbers and reportedly started dating. So by the time she was twenty years old, Beyoncé had helped popularize a certain kind of confidence, while quietly building relationships in private. And in time, with the support of her parents, it would help establish her move towards a solo career.

* * * * *

In a VH1 special, seventeen-year-old twins – Stacey and Tracey – identified themselves as Destiny's Child superfans. They imbibed Beyoncé's self-love messaging, as delivered through single 'Bootylicious'. 'I most definitely love "Bootylicious", because it makes me feel like, "OK – you don't have to be that perfect size six or size two,"' Tracey said, as the pair sat in a shared bedroom covered floor to ceiling in Destiny's Child posters. 'You can love yourself and still be that wonderful, beautiful person you are.' Stacey added: 'You can be independent. You don't have to depend on anybody but yourself. It's just empowerment, for everybody.' For these two Black girls from Detroit, Beyoncé embodied more than a fount of musical skill. She represented acceptance.

Here's the thing: it is obvious that Beyoncé's body type – an hourglass figure – is considered ideal by US beauty standards. But with 'Bootylicious', she also amplified a term for a certain pride in being curvier, or what Black Americans would term 'thick'. It would take another 15 years for this body type to land in the mainstream, popularized by Armenian-American showbiz family the Kardashians. Typically, a white-passing family would be credited with pushing an aesthetic long-valorized by Black and Latinx people into an ideal. Nonetheless, the word bootylicious became a sort of shorthand for 'my body is mine, and that's OK'. Beyoncé has said that she wrote the song after her own struggle. As she told *Cosmopolitan* in 2008, 'I had gained a little weight, and I was making fun of it.'

Between the drastic diet she underwent as a teen and the extreme food plan she described in 2018's Netflix documentary about the making of her Coachella headline performance, her issues with body image run on multiple levels. To fans, though, none of this appeared on the surface. She seemed resolutely unflappable and able to lead them. She emanated an inspiring perspective. And, in 2008, the word bootylicious was added to the *Oxford English Dictionary* (albeit with a somewhat dubious definition, limited to attractiveness rather than stressing empowerment). In a 2001 MTV interview with Kelly and Michelle, as part of a documentary series, Beyoncé said she wrote the song to show listeners that she and her bandmates were 'regular' people, too. 'We go through feeling insecure about not being the typical body type – that's why we wrote "Bootylicious", to make people feel good about themselves, no matter how they look.'

And it worked. In the same documentary series, a white English fan interviewed after Destiny's Child's BRIT Awards performance in 2001 echoed the same sense of belonging heard from Stacey and Tracey. 'I think [Destiny's Child] are just the best,' she said, beaming and with a resolute calm in her voice. 'I mean, things like "Independent Women" – it's so brilliant. Everyone loves it; everyone says, "you wrote that song for me". And it's true.' That, surely, captured the essence of Destiny's Child's crossover ability.

The group's first and second albums provided the foundation upon which Beyoncé built that wider audience and *Survivor* cemented it. The singer has said she was nineteen years old when she wrote 'Independent Women', tapping into the momentum of songs such as 'Bills, Bills, Bills' to hit upon a universally inspirational tone. Beyoncé now recognized that Destiny's Child could speak to people of all genders and ethnicities. Yes, 'Bug a Boo' and 'Bills' were recorded with other Black women in mind – they're talking to listeners almost in a code based on shared experience.

But with 'Independent Women' Beyoncé savvily proved that she and her bandmates could broaden their appeal while still sounding true to themselves. Their fast-paced vocals delivered over hip-hop beats could remain similar from one album to the next, even if the lens through which their songs were viewed widened. They didn't have to compromise on authenticity. And, as she moved into her early twenties with *Survivor*, Beyoncé continued to rack up songwriting and vocal production credits. 'I actually wrote and produced "Independent Women" and "Jumpin, Jumpin" and eight other songs on [*The Writing's on the Wall*],' she said, in an early 2000s VH1 broadcast. 'It's really cool when you write your own songs because people can relate to you when they see you onstage. They know that it's personal.' This may sound like a basic concept, but it gets straight to the core of her connection with Destiny's Child's fans. When her fans sang words that she had written, it fortified the link between group and audience. And Beyoncé had not only her parents but also her own resolve to thank for this foresight.

* * * * *

Tina Knowles-Lawson is today practically famous in her own right. She gives solo interviews, wins leadership awards, commands the attention of thousands of Instagram followers – even though she no longer works for her eldest daughter. She progressed from being simply Beyoncé's childhood champion to the official stylist for Girls Tyme and Destiny's Child in the 1990s (which is how most people around the world were introduced to Tina). In the decades since, her presence in Beyoncé's life has continued to loom large, a mother figure extending her warm embrace to each and every fan.

Crucially, as Beyoncé blossomed into adulthood, she turned to her mother as a role model. Tina had shown her daughter the importance of being both business-minded and economically self-sufficient, as well as the power of a well-manicured, feminine image. Without her continual support, the Beyoncé we see today may never have materialized.

Tina had been a secretary at a credit card company when she met Mathew, lacking a university degree but able to nimbly move between skill sets and locations. When Beyoncé was only a couple of months old, Tina made a point of starting her own business in a bid to maintain financial independence. Starting out as a homeworking hairstylist, by 1985 she had opened her own salon, Headliners. At the time, Mathew Knowles was earning a six-figure salary, and Tina had no urgent need to find work. She is, however, like her daughter, a natural grafter.

Her own mother had always told her to keep something for herself in any romantic relationship – never to be completely reliant on a future husband. To do so, Tina's mother emphasized working for yourself. Beyoncé's grandmother didn't get to enjoy the luxury of raising her children with money to spare, but she set an example nonetheless. At a 2019 conference for young women of colour, Tina summed up those lessons: 'My mom taught me how to take nothing and turn it into something – and to never give up.'

So, when Destiny's Child set the 'Bills, Bills, Bills' music video in a hairdresser's, they were paying their respects to both Headliners and Tina's hard work. Beyoncé often spoke about the connection hairstylists establish with regular customers, and how the salon becomes a congregation point for personal stories and mutual support. Women sharing their romantic woes, triumphs and complications would directly feed into Destiny's Child's music.

But Tina displayed a very particular harmony between being business-minded – shrewd, even – and maintaining a delicate sense of care for others. Beyoncé would channel this dichotomy from her teens onward. As Destiny's Child grew in popularity, she and her family donated $1.5 million in 2002, to help build the $2 million Knowles-Rowland Center for Youth. The facility at St. John's Downtown United Methodist Church, Beyoncé's childhood church, would become the site for the collection and sorting of donations for those impacted by Hurricane Katrina a few years later.

With generosity came savviness; Beyoncé was also developing her mother's knack for sniffing out bullshit and learning to stand up for herself. 'I was too young,' she said in 2002, of debut album *Destiny's Child*. 'I didn't know I was supposed to get percentages and credit [for writing and producing].' By album two, she was channelling her mother's 'make it work' philosophy behind the scenes. 'I could produce with just us in the studio – we really didn't need anybody else.' And by *Survivor*, she said she realized she could be, and should be, getting credit. Asked if it was harder for her to get those producer credits as a woman, she laughed: 'I think being a young Black woman made it a lot harder.' Chances are, millions still don't realize she put in work on *Destiny's Child* that has gone uncredited to this day.

Beyoncé's hyper-feminine, meticulously groomed appearance, the physical essence of her image-building, also rests on a base laid by her mother. With her long, wavy hair and often red-stained lips, Tina typifies a certain – and Southern – gender ideal. Beyoncé has gone on to carry that mantle, and proudly. She is often criticized for appearing 'too sexual' or too provocatively dressed, or too quick to 'flaunt' her figure. Rather, you could say that she chooses to treat her body as a site of expression, through clothing, styling and grooming. No doubt, she sees how her appearance can be turned into a commodity – her later move into designing clothing proves this alone.

But Beyoncé also shows the public that the typically feminine can sit alongside what we often interpret as masculine strength: business savvy, a tightly gripped control, a steely determination. Mathew Knowles too contributed to this fortitude in his daughter. His role as her manager was openly derided, especially in the wake of the lawsuits filed by LaTavia Roberson and LeToya Luckett. Still, Mathew does deserve credit for noticing in his daughter the roar of tenacity and coaxing it from her for years. It would not be an exaggeration to say that he worked her nearly to the bone during her childhood and teens. His relentless drive for success – a sort of bottomless pit fed only by more work and more results – derived from his scrabble upwards from poverty to starched shirts in the corporate world.

When, then, his daughter showed promise he pulled from her a dedication to working hard, consistently. By her late teens, she had committed to a schedule and pace that would send heads spinning. Soon, Destiny's Child became a product beyond just their music. Young fans today may laugh at clips showing Destiny's Child in adverts, but for Mathew in the early 2000s, they were big business. 'We were about branding, not just the music,' Mathew said, in 2019, emphasizing how he used his sales background to wrangle endorsements for the group. 'No one was really doing that. We had brand partners [such as] L'Oréal, Nintendo, American Express.' Here, Mathew left his mark, inky and distinct. Beyoncé was quickly learning that she was not only a person but also a product.

During her teens and early twenties, she saw how her image could be used to bulk out another company's bottom line. And you could easily assume that, driven by her father's focus on making Destiny's Child stand out, she felt she was always in competition with her peers in the industry. For a young performer, those are jarring moments to process and ones which may not make sense without the benefit of long experience in the business.

She would soon carry all of this information as she walked towards a career cliff edge, preparing to jump off into the unknown. After more than ten years in a group, she was about to strike out on her own. Beyoncé had always previously told inquiring reporters that there were no plans for anyone in Destiny's Child to record as a solo artist, but by 2003, that was no longer the case. She was strong enough, by then, to try and stand without the support of two bandmates. She was going solo.

V.

'I Know It's Gonna Be Great'

It was already quite the résumé. Before her twenty-second birthday, Beyoncé had pulled off a feat of accomplishments dizzying enough to make you want to sit down for a bit. She had led Destiny's Child to five Grammy award victories, millions in sales and record-breaking successes – among them, gathering up the most Billboard Hot 100 number 1s for any girl group, ever, and being the only all-woman group to simultaneously top both the UK and US singles charts with the same song.

As with many a child star, she could have quite happily shimmied away from the glow of stage spotlights and settled into a regular life. But that would never do. Granted, in several early interviews, Destiny's Child had insisted that no one harboured a desire to go solo – but by the time the group had shrunk to a trio, they had changed their minds. Beyoncé, Michelle and Kelly worked out a plan to put out solo albums, one after the other, following the May 2001 release of *Survivor*. In June 2003, sandwiched between Williams's well-received gospel offering and Rowland's take on pop and R&B, came Beyoncé's first foray into the world of the solo artist.

Yet this period in Beyoncé's life isn't merely shaped by the build-up to, and reception of, her blockbuster debut album,

Dangerously in Love. No doubt, the grit and energy she hammered into the album is a testament to her continued laser-sharp focus, a concentration that could cut glass. Musically, however, she took risks that may not have been as apparent at the time. By doing so, she risked stumbling backwards just as her career as part of a group was skyrocketing. These early years of her solo work instead drew a line in the sand between the Beyoncé the public had known as a child, and the Beyoncé brand that would eventually swell to an almost uncontainable force. Beyoncé still spoke openly to the press, galloping around on the promotional trail as she was obliged to do. An overarching sense of trying to reconcile the different parts of her persona typified this time.

She was to be sexy, but not too much. She was meant to prove herself, even to those who had no interest in taking her seriously. She would branch out into acting, with mixed results. And yet, she kept pushing, working non-stop, hinting at her exhaustion in snatches of candid moments. Overall, she had not yet broken away from the protection and influence of her parents – she was, however, beginning to shove against the bounds of her working relationship with her father in particular. They were still a team, though. At this stage, she needed all the support she could muster. After all, she wanted to be the biggest and the best. The only question remaining was whether the world would accept her as such.

* * * * *

While making the video for her first solo single, Beyoncé seemed reinforced with steel. She appeared nervous and excited, sometimes breathlessly so, but approached the 'Crazy in Love' music video shoot with almost unshakeable mettle. It was early 2003, on one of those Los Angeles days where the winter sun tempts you out and dares you to stick to wearing just one layer by dusk. Following her guest appearance on Jay-Z's track "03 Bonnie & Clyde' the year before, they joined forces again. Rumours of their romance swirled, but she wouldn't answer direct questions about it.

Director Jake Nava, who would become a long-time Beyoncé collaborator, was working with the star for the first time. 'Crazy in Love' carried a hefty burden, serving as an introduction to a newly polished look and sound for Beyoncé. And so her and Nava's concept rested on marrying ragged-edged concrete street scenes with flowing, lavish silks – Versace, naturally – worn by Beyoncé and her dancers, in a series of locations. You could tell Beyoncé was a solo novice. Nava barked both orders and encouragement at her during takes, willing her to bend her body closer to the ground, along knee-scraping gravel, or applauding her for a saucy look thrown down the lens. She complied, channelling her years of experience on camera into another slowly arched back here, a pavement-stomping strut there.

'I'm twenty-one now,' she said, beaming as she wrapped herself in the warmth of a robe between scenes. 'And I wanted to make that statement – but in a very classy way.' By 'that statement' she referred to the notion of unquestionable adulthood. At that age, you can pretty much do it all: drink, drive, fornicate, marry, go to war. In Beyoncé's eyes, turning twenty-one would allow her to acknowledge her womanhood, tangled up in desire and power and ambition. Of the video, she then simply said: 'I know it's gonna be great.'

Fans in the 2020s express being knocked sideways by the nonchalance of that statement, understanding how her career would grow. At the time, though, she was just a precocious, clear-headed young woman. 'She knows what she wants,' Nava said, behind the scenes on the shoot. 'I'm really impressed by her focus and her vision, for someone of her age.' Then he added: 'But not really surprised, because that's why she is who she is.' Nava here captures an intrinsic part of Beyoncé's success: she could *visualize* what she wanted and would do anything to render that vision a reality. In a way, her entire childhood had braced Beyoncé for the impact of her early twenties. Working from a young age in an industry shaped by other stakeholders first made her aware of herself not only as a little girl in Houston but also as a person housing a voice that could be both a product and a tool. She learned to see outside herself, to perceive herself through the eyes of adults – often, the audience and stakeholders she strained to impress.

As a by-product of working consistently from a young age, aiming an abundance of energy at signing a record deal, Beyoncé became different from most of her peers. She no doubt bore some scars from a childhood spent racing towards adult ambition. On the BBC programme *The Graham Norton Show* in 2003, she explained: 'I was very focused at a young age. I was a little strange.' That term, 'a little strange', can be read as code for 'I was not like other children my age.' There's proof of that in how Beyoncé approached her work in her early twenties. She had grown up fast in showbiz. But, unusually, once she'd reached her childhood goals – a record deal, a headline tour, the Grammy awards – she continued to grow. She learned to slice into and dismantle obstacles that stood in the way of the next ream of accomplishments.

As a solo star, those obstacles took the form of doubt from critics and uncertainty from fans of Destiny's Child, nervous about the group's future. They took the form of wink-wink jabs under the ribs wheeled out by some in the media, suggesting Beyoncé could not pull off a career on her own. Those commentators may have decided that she was just one of many pretty young women who'd fade into nothing in a few years, replaced by another long-haired, glowy-skinned nymph ready for the spotlight. Beyoncé conquered those obstacles methodically. She drew on internal reserves of energy and the vim of her support structure, pushing through what could have become stultifying routine. Perhaps she forged ahead with her vision for *Dangerously in Love* so determinedly because it was not the first time she had considered a working life without Destiny's Child.

According to J. Randy Taraborrelli's 2015 biography, Beyoncé had come close to leaving Destiny's Child much earlier than fans would know. By his account, in the final weeks of 1999, LaTavia Roberson and LeToya Luckett had sent legal letters to Mathew Knowles, affirming their desire to end their management contracts with him. These notices stung Beyoncé, landing like a sharp slap making contact with her, her father and her best friend, Kelly Rowland. And so, still a teen, she thought aloud about both her and Kelly going solo, to finally shake off the 'drama' of the group's founding members. She went so far as to fax a letter to Don Ienner, then-president of Sony, professing her intention to go solo. It was only thanks to Tina's nimble thinking that Beyoncé stuck with Destiny's Child. Her mother drove the hunt for the two newcomers who would introduce themselves to the world in the 'Say My Name' music video. Crisis averted. But that near-decision foretold how steady Beyoncé's resolve could be, even as a very young adult. Before sharing her solo album statement with the world, she applied that resolve to another venture. Beyoncé set her sights on Hollywood.

* * * * *

Now, a moment's silence for the musicians who've leapt shakily from pop's well-worn path and chucked themselves into the unknown of acting. There are less public ways to fall flat on one's face. And in plenty of cases, from rapper LL Cool J to Mariah Carey, it just takes the right script (and an element of sympathy from viewers and critics) to pull it off. At the turn of the twenty-first century, when Beyoncé limbered up for this jump, she faced the judgement of a particularly cruel celebrity press.

Gossip magazines, and later gossip blogs, had not quite yet hit the crescendo of hysterical cackling and brow-waggling that would define the end of that first decade of the 2000s. Paparazzi upskirt photos of famous, young white women folding their warmly tanned limbs into saloon cars after boozy nights out had not fully become considered 'normal' rather than 'invasive, weird and unnecessary'. As a young Black woman, Beyoncé occupied a very specific place in the eyes of the mainstream press.

There was an expectation that she would stay in her lane. Before she and her bandmates had even released *Survivor* in 2001, they had already felt the wrath of the tabloid press and celebrity TV reporters. Entire *Saturday Night Live* sketches were dedicated to skewering Destiny's Child by likening them to a cut-throat episode of desert-island endurance reality show *Survivor*. (That barb, of course, compelled Beyoncé to write a song of the same name.) From MTV News to E! Entertainment, regular segments saw fit to pick at celebrities' private lives. Many of those shows ran on the finest dusting of fact, scattered by 'unnamed sources'. Beyoncé worried about what her fans might think when they learned about her first acting role via those entertainment channels. And, as she would write in *Soul Survivors*, the part itself hardly eased her concerns.

You see, director Robert Townsend had sought Beyoncé to play the titular lead in the made-for-MTV film *Carmen: A Hip Hopera*. In addition to singing and rapping, she would have to embody a hypersexual character. Beyoncé went so far as to describe Townsend's original Carmen as 'pure evil' with 'no redeeming qualities'. Hardly the best role with which to keep a tween audience sweet. In the end, with some gentle coaxing, she persuaded Townsend to tone down some of Carmen's more salacious scenes and lines. Nonetheless, this first role saw Beyoncé wrestle with the image she projected – sultry, ballsy, always 'on' – with her real character. 'It was very interesting playing Carmen because I'm so not like her,' Beyoncé said in 2001, laughing. 'As far as her flirting and her... sexy... she's just such a little flirt.' And she giggled again.

But, again and again, from her 2002 supporting role as Foxxy Cleopatra in *Austin Powers in Goldmember* to her starring role opposite Cuba Gooding Jr. in 2003's gospel feel-good flick *The Fighting Temptations*, her sex appeal sat at the core of her casting. Over the next few years, this fixation on her body's curves, the cut of performance outfits and the thrust of her dancing would become a cross to bear.

She did her best with both her limited acting experience and the (mostly) limiting ingénue characters into which she was meant to pour some life. More often, scathing reviews would pan the storylines themselves – notably, for *The Fighting Temptations* – rather than her foray into the acting world. She battled the ever-present dilemma for Black actresses: to be considered 'real' to Black audiences while marketable to white ones. The media critic of the *Chicago Tribune* summarized, unwittingly, the racial gap between these worlds in his review of *Carmen*.

'MTV's promotional wisdom did not include sending me a screening tape of the movie,' he wrote, haughtily, 'but the musical stars include these people I've heard of if I haven't actually heard,' before listing Beyoncé's name alongside those of Da Brat and Mos Def (now known as Yasiin Bey). As a pop star, Beyoncé had steamrollered Destiny's Child into the centre of musical youth culture. She hadn't managed yet to shake 'urban' labelling, but was not considered as 'niche' as some of the rappers the *Tribune* professed not to have heard by 2001 when several had been working for over a decade.

But Beyoncé still had to prove her place in the spotlight. In acting, she didn't do too badly. With her solo career, she shot off to a rocket-fuelled start. *Dangerously in Love* debuted at the top of the Billboard 200 chart, sliding beneath R&B singer Ashanti in its second week. It spent five weeks in peak position on the UK Official Album Chart. Singles 'Crazy in Love' and 'Baby Boy' each topped the Billboard Hot 100 – 'Crazy in Love' pulled off that feat based on radio airplay alone (the Hot 100 chart is compiled from sales numbers, streaming and airplay, rather than sales alone, allowing the single to hit the top spot before being available in retail outlets). And, 12 years later, the album surpassed 5 million in cumulative US sales.

Two anecdotes sum up how, even with this commercial success, Beyoncé was still nowhere near icon status. The first is one click away, in the *New York Times* digital archive. Their 2003 review of *Dangerously in Love* pitted Beyoncé against her chart rival. Its headline read: 'The Solo Beyoncé: She's No Ashanti', and critic Kelefa Sanneh went on to wonder if the album provided 'proof that she isn't quite as versatile as she seemed'.

The second anecdote is one that Beyoncé often recounts as she catches her breath onstage between songs. In 2011, during the taping of a concert at New York City's Roseland Ballroom, she recalled taking her first album to Sony, finished, for them to hear: 'I put my heart and my soul into *Dangerously in Love*. And after playing my records for the record label they told me I didn't have one hit single,' she said, pausing before listing 'Dangerously in Love', 'Me, Myself and I', 'Baby Boy', 'Naughty Girl' and 'Crazy in Love'. '[They] told me, "I'm sorry, Beyoncé, but I don't hear one hit single." I guess they were right. I had five.'

VI.

The Hustle and Hive

On a Sunday evening in mid-May 2005, Destiny's Child bounced onstage in Norway, buoyed by the piercing screams of 5,500 fans. The trio harmonized almost as one voice, standing practically cheek to cheek with their glowing skin and hair catching a light further reflected by their matching copper and black diamanté-panelled dresses. Beyoncé wrapped an arm around Michelle Williams's waist, while Williams rested her hand on Kelly Rowland's torso, eyes closed or heads flung back in visible elation. This was the first night of the European leg of their McDonald's-sponsored tour: 'Destiny Fulfilled… and Lovin' It'. Corporate ties aside (they would end the night thanking the fast-food behemoth), the show blasted out full-on glamour. Tina had designed all the group's outfits, in another savvy deal. In this case, the clothing served as free advertising for Beyoncé and her mother's joint clothing line, House of Deréon, named after Tina's late mother. For fans, though, this was finally a chance to see the group reunited.

After stepping aside to record and release their solo albums, they had linked arms again, coming back – as promised – on the fourth studio album, *Destiny Fulfilled*. But its title ought to have hinted at the end of the line for new Destiny's Child music, a sense of contentment implied in that expression of fulfilment. Still, many fans weren't ready for that hint to be made real.

About a month after that concert in Oslo, on 11 June 2005, Destiny's Child confirmed they were disbanding. During a raucous show played to a 16,000-strong crowd in Barcelona, Kelly Rowland reportedly announced their plans to go their separate ways when the 'Destiny Fulfilled' tour would come to a stop in North America in September. For all the coy answers Beyoncé had given in previous interviews, about the chances of more Destiny's Child music after *Destiny Fulfilled*, the choice had been made.

Officially, after the Barcelona show, they shared this statement: 'We have been working together as Destiny's Child since we were nine, and touring together since we were fourteen. After a lot of discussion and some deep soul searching, we realized that our current tour has given us the opportunity to leave Destiny's Child on a high note, united in our friendship and filled with an overwhelming gratitude for our music, our fans, and each other.' After going on to describe regrouping for *Destiny Fulfilled* as a 'time of natural growth for us', the group ended their note – graciously, of course – by thanking the fans. This marked the complete end of Beyoncé's working life with the hovering safety net of bandmates, ready to catch her at a mid-sentence stumble during an interview, or a missed cue onstage. Now, with the added pressure to better her debut *Dangerously in Love*, she was truly on her own.

A relentless pace marked the five years between Destiny's Child's last tour and the lead-up towards the only career hiatus Beyoncé would take. In that time, she balanced performance with more charitable projects. Just as she had worked to prove Destiny's Child deserved their place in the upper echelons of pop and R&B, Beyoncé would have to do the same for herself. And even with the success she had already established, it would be no cakewalk.

* * * * *

Reporter Liam Bartlett thought he could make sense of how Beyoncé saw herself. As the host delivering the cold open for a *60 Minutes Australia* TV news segment, he summed the star up as 'a prime example of bootylicious', taking care to add that that was how she described herself. Next: 'beautiful, bountiful, bounceable', as though he were casually recalling the contours of a plastic toy for children. At one point during the pre-taped broadcast, he went so far as to exalt how she seemed to transform – accompanied with a 'wow' – into an 'erotic, uninhibited showgirl' who was 'unleashed'.

Watching Bartlett try to translate Beyoncé's appeal for a mainstream Australian audience feels like watching someone attempt to break her down, joint by joint, into a scattered pile of parts to assemble. Bartlett went on to make Beyoncé laugh during their conversation, and they appeared to partake in a perfectly pleasant interview. But his voiceover segments perfectly illustrate the double-bind she had found herself in at the start of her solo career. In Destiny's Child, she and the girls had often been made to answer for their tight leather trousers and crop tops, or blown-out 'Texas' hair. The subtext rang loud: 'you young ladies look too grown for your age'. *Dangerously in Love* had debuted an adult Beyoncé, dancing in heels while the fluttering hemlines of minidresses skipped over her thighs. To her, these were stage costumes, often signed off or devised by her mother.

But to outsiders, Beyoncé's body became a site of an almost tortuous tug-of-war. On one side, cultural norms around objectifying women made it easy for viewers to focus on her perceived eroticism with little regard for her music. On the other, critics tried to compute a churchgoing, family-oriented young woman with the same person who arched her back on dark sand, wearing a gilded bra top and miniskirt in the video for 'Baby Boy'. There was no room for nuance, for an acceptance that she could be composed of many facets at once.

Beyoncé was, let's be clear, still devoted to her faith. In September 2005, she, her family and Kelly Rowland founded the Survivor Foundation, to help rehouse those displaced by Hurricane Katrina. She took on several anti-hunger initiatives around this time, imploring fans in 2006 to donate non-perishable food at her concerts as well as partnering with several charities on a digital, global food drive pegged to her 'Beyoncé Experience' tour in 2007. Over time, she would place and amplify this work under her 'BeyGood' brand.

Yet her sexuality came to define the start of her solo career. And it was nigh on entirely misunderstood. At this time the cultural gatekeepers were not young women like her, who would have well understood the steps you trace from teendom to a profound mastery of your own desires, self-image and determination of self-worth. Of course,

Beyoncé had grown up hearing that she was a pretty girl and later a beautiful woman. But because she embodied a different persona onstage, she didn't have to make the direct connection between her private self – the seemingly pious, shy young woman – and her public self, read as raunchy, and in possession of an almost pulsing sensuality. She knew she could be both at once, even though that may have confounded her peers and critics.

'Part of her wide appeal is that she is both wholesome and sexy at the same time,' wrote a journalist in 2004, for *Texas Monthly* magazine. 'She's also mysteriously pan-racial – she's Black, but with her blond locks and golden skin, she could be just about any color.' During the photoshoot for that same story, the photographer objectified Beyoncé more than once. 'You're way too curvy for *Texas Monthly*,' he reportedly said at one point, which the journalist interpreted as a joke while he watched the shoot. An exchange followed, with the photographer imploring Beyoncé to position herself without jutting out a hip and placing her hand on it (her onstage trademark pose, even now after all these years). She declined. Not long after, the photographer gave a direction: 'easy on the smoulder.' This trend ran through so many of her press appearances, a young woman in her early twenties considered fodder for fantasies projected out into the heavens. In a *Rolling Stone* interview, writer and podcaster Touré spent a substantial chunk of his wordcount on descriptions of her body, a languid eye cast over her with more than a hint of drooling to boot.

'She has golden skin, three small birthmarks on her face, perfect teeth and a dancer's posture,' he wrote, within

Destiny's Child performing in their original four-piece formation,
in California in May 1998. Tina Knowles designed many
of the group's stage costumes. L-R: LaTavia Roberson (just seen),
Beyoncé Knowles, Kelly Rowland and LeToya Luckett.

TOP – Destiny's Child with their very first awards:
three gongs won at the 1998 Lady of Soul Awards. LaTavia dedicated
the award to the band's first manager, Andretta Tillman.

ABOVE – A new Destiny's Child configuration emerges. Beyoncé and Kelly
are joined by members Farrah Franklin (centre R) and Michelle Williams (R),
posing during MTV's Spring Break 2000 in Cancún, Mexico.

Beyoncé on the promotional trail with Destiny's Child in November 2000,
at New York City's Apollo Theater.

After Farrah's departure, Destiny's Child became a trio. Here, they stand with the trophies won at 2001's 43rd annual Grammy Awards, in Los Angeles.

An early meeting between Destiny's Child and rapper Jay-Z,
in New York City in January 2001. Beyoncé and Jay-Z would not go public
as a couple until 2004, after collaborating on two singles in 2002 and 2003.

Backstage at the 2004 Grammy Awards, Beyoncé holds her five trophies. They were her first Grammys as a solo performer.

The singer duets with Prince at the 2004 Grammy Awards. Later she would say that pulling this face was Prince's idea, whispered just before they went onstage.

Beyoncé as Etta James, in the 2008 film *Cadillac Records*. She executive-produced the multi-character music biopic, via her company Parkwood Entertainment.

In June 2009, Beyoncé helped kick off an annual US hunger-relief initiative. Since her time in Destiny's Child, she has donated to and spread awareness of various charitable projects, focusing on natural disaster survivors, women living with substance-use disorders and more.

A glimpse of the star's perspective: Beyoncé greets fans along
the red carpet at the August 2014 MTV Video Music Awards in Los Angeles.

TOP – Beyoncé begins the Australian leg of her mammoth *I Am...* world tour, in September 2009 in Melbourne. The end of this tour marked a period of reflection and the start of a (brief) work hiatus.

ABOVE – Debuting single 'Formation', Beyoncé performs during Coldplay's Super Bowl half-time show in February 2016. Months later, she would release groundbreaking visual album *Lemonade*.

TOP – Family life has anchored much of Beyoncé's career to date. Here, her father – and then-manager – Mathew Knowles holds her close in Houston in 2001, on a Destiny's Child photoshoot.

ABOVE – Solange (L), Beyoncé's younger sister, has become a recording artist in her own right, while their mother, Tina (R), cultivates her own audience on social media and in business. They stand together in 2006, at a Chicago launch of Beyoncé and Tina's House of Deréon clothing line.

Now married, Jay-Z and Beyoncé share a kiss onstage during the 2014 MTV Music Video Awards in California, as Beyoncé receives her Michael Jackson Video Vanguard Award. The couple hold their firstborn daughter, Blue Ivy Carter.

Beyoncé and Jay-Z take part in the second line parade during Solange and her husband Alan Ferguson's wedding. The second line is a New Orleans, Louisiana tradition.

A brief moment of quiet before the red carpet chaos:
Beyoncé walks her daughter Blue Ivy into the 2016 MTV Video Music Awards
at Madison Square Garden in New York City.

reason. To read the next line, however, knowing it went past the eyes of several editors before landing on the page, may give you pause: 'And her tight jeans reveal her to be a healthy girl, someone the brothers would call thick, with a booming system in the back.' At the time, comparing Beyoncé's bottom to an inanimate object was the norm. And that norm extended not only to how pop culture viewed women's bodies, but to how male journalists could pour their personal feelings into their professional copy (in 2019, a former co-worker accused Touré of past sexual harassment, which he described as 'edgy and crass banter' in his apology statement).

Luckily, Beyoncé had devised a clever method to cleave apart those sides of her persona. Well, it would perhaps be more accurate to give that credit to her cousin, and long-time former personal assistant, Angie Beyince. She bestowed her cousin's stage persona with the name Sasha Fierce. Wrapping his mind around how polite and quiet Beyoncé was in person, interviewer Liam Bartlett asked her directly about her alter ego: 'The leather-clad' – and then he hissed out the following sibilant – 'ssssex machine, that's Sasha?' he asked. 'Can we interview Sasha?'

But that's not how it worked. His questioning demonstrates how this alter ego was readily misunderstood. Sasha was for the stage and the video set, only. 'When I perform,' Beyoncé said in 2004, 'this confidence and this sexiness and this whatever it is that I'm completely not just happens. And you feel it, and you just start wildin' and doin' stuff that don't even make sense, like the spirit takes over.' She would find herself explaining the logic behind Sasha repeatedly.

Musically, Sasha allowed her to explore terrain that would have been off-limits to Beyoncé.

And it is worth pausing for a moment to recall what she was up against. Though she had sold millions of records, Beyoncé had already taken risks on her debut album. The horn-flecked, retro-leaning sound of lead single 'Crazy in Love' was no sure thing. In fact, as the song's producer Rich Harrison remembered, Beyoncé almost walked away from the seventies-sampling beat he'd put together, lifting horns from Chicago soul outfit The Chi-Lites. That brass – later, a world-famous riff – hadn't fit the sound of 2002-going-on-2003. And only when Harrison worked on a hook (Beyoncé gave him a deadline of a couple of hours, while he was hungover in the studio no less) did Beyoncé come on board with the song.

By the time she released *B'Day*, her second studio album, in 2006 she had imbibed the potency of that subtly retro sound. Horns paraded over click-click-clickety percussion on the enormous-sounding single 'Freakum Dress' (an ode to that one party dress a woman might keep on reserve, even when she's reclined into coupled-up domesticity). Harmonized horns soared into a crescendo before giving way to stripped-back drums on 'Green Light', a single that waves an impatient hand at a man dilly-dallying before leaving a romantic relationship for good. And a delicious bassline-drenched 'Déjà Vu', featuring another star turn by Beyoncé's future husband, Jay-Z.

Commercially, she proved this style could work. *B'Day* debuted at number 1, as did *I Am... Sasha Fierce*, her more ambitious (and just-a-little-too-long) double album in 2008. At the time, best-selling music in the US ran the gamut from the wet indie-pop of Daniel Powter's 'Bad Day' and near-R&B by non-Black artists over fizzing synths – think Nelly Furtado or Justin Timberlake – to Akon's sing-song R&B, stuffed with rap features. Beyond the charts, and the storied realm of traditional radio, a coalition of fans was growing. Initially, they were unknown to outsiders. With time came global recognition, and a name: the BeyHive.

* * * * *

Sisa Zekani, now twenty-seven, often felt like an outsider during his childhood. As a self-proclaimed 'visibly queer kid' in Port Elizabeth, South Africa, he often spent time alone, indoors, to swerve the lingering threat of bullies. 'I'd always been fascinated by fabulous women and beauty,' he says, 'so I spent most of my childhood seeking them out.' And that meant taking in plenty of TV, pop radio and flicking through magazines.

'But something about the "Crazy in Love" video hit me differently,' he said. Sisa, like so many millennial Beyoncé fans, knew of Destiny's Child. Yet it was her solo work that propelled the star towards an almost otherworldly presence in his life. Today, Sisa's online commentary about Beyoncé can pick up hundreds of thousands of interactions on Twitter. A platinum tweet is just about his bread and butter, but he gained his footing in many of the other online spaces that saw thousands of fans dedicate hours to dissecting, appreciating and championing her work.

He encapsulates so much about not only Beyoncé's appeal but also her global impact. The BeyHive is considered a formidable force for this exact reason. In many respects, that a South African boy found kinship with so many unseen global peers grounds Beyoncé's status as a twentieth-century talent who leapt into the twenty-first century. Twitter may now be the main battleground for stan face-offs (although Sisa does not identify as a stan, nor would I call him one). But years ago, the BeyHive as we know it multiplied in lesser-known corners of the internet.

'I'm old enough to remember when urban blog comment sections and forums like Beyoncé World, That Grape Juice and Sandra Rose were at their popularity peak,' Sisa says. After finding the blogs by chance – he'd been looking for a Beyoncé photo to set as his computer background screen – their comments sections sucked him in. 'I was completely enamoured with the way they spoke, the things they argued about and how knowledgeable everyone seemed to be on pop culture in general.' He practically gorged himself on Beyoncé-related facts as a high-schooler. Years later, he comfortably discusses her 'eras' (a fan term for career stages) and how he found community in those spaces.

The BeyHive has taken on many forms online. Within years, it evolved from those early forums that Sisa mentioned – sites like BeyonceWorld.net, from which now-defunct The Beyhive.com was spawned – to a constellation of sites and social media accounts on several platforms. But the individual websites and Twitter accounts are perhaps less important. What matters is their overall impact, a thundering roar of bee emojis, social media responses, coordinated campaigns to buy her music and push their idol up the charts. As such, Beyoncé fans have earned a reputation for being too protective of their 'fave'. A 2014 *Saturday Night Live* sketch parodied the BeyHive, recasting them as the Beygency, who would hunt down anyone who so much as made a mild criticism of the star. It's not far off from what happens in real life. But a frequently made mistake should be noted – following the correct pronunciation of Beyoncé's name the pun fails, becoming the 'Bee-gency' rather than 'Bay-gency'.

TheBeyHive.com founder Cody L. wondered, in 2016, how the presence of the 'hive' might feel to Beyoncé herself. 'That's got to be such an amazing feeling, a scary feeling, to be an artist knowing if someone says something about you, there are a million people who are going to shut shit down,' he said. To Sisa, this protectiveness stems less from some cultish hysteria than from a desire to stand up for a Black woman who is often publicly maligned. As he puts it, simply: 'She's the most visible Black woman in the world.'

While the BeyHive grew, Beyoncé still tussled for her seat at the head of the pop-culture table. So, to assess her fandom only through the headlines it generated in later years does its core a disservice. In 2008, when blog commenters went deep on her videos, she was not yet an unquestionable force in music. But the fervour of their passion, their framing of her as practically a hobby, set a template. Fans of singers such as Lady Gaga, Rihanna, Ariana Grande, Selena Gomez and others learned many a technique from Beyoncé's hive.

Yet, it is the connections, crisscrossing over the planet, that lend the BeyHive its affectionate place in the hearts of fans. 'Most parents don't think boys should play with dolls and they share the same sentiments about playing with female pop stars,' Sisa says. His Beyoncé obsession became a vector for his queerness and a sense of commonality. 'I spent a lot of time on the forums with other gay people from all around the world, and I learned all the gay slang (reading, shade, receipts etc.), where to find more Beyoncé-related information and more people in the community.' Now, he says he's 'an advocate of how much you can learn from art if you care enough to do the research.' Fitting, for fans of an artist who meticulously studied her way to performance perfection.

VII.

A Hard Year

Beyoncé was tired. And fair enough – wouldn't you be? By the February 2010 end of her 'I Am...' world tour, a six-leg, 11-month stretch of more than 100 performances, she was, by her own admission, overworked. She had gone through major life changes and not necessarily let them sink in. She and Jay-Z had married in a secret ceremony in 2008 after finally going public as a couple on an MTV red carpet in 2004. Then: back to work. Later she would describe this period – the whirlwind whipping her through the promotion of her third solo studio album – as a bit of a blur. 'You're getting awards, and people are saying how much they respect you and... I couldn't even hear it anymore,' she remembered, finding her mind racing to the 'next video, next single, next tour'. She had to stop.

In many ways, 2009 had felt like the most momentous year in her working life to date. 'I've always worked hard, but I feel like I worked harder this past year than I have since I was just starting out,' she said, in 2010. In fairness, her ten Grammy nominations showed off the fruits of her labour, making her that year's most-nominated artist going into the 2010 awards ceremony.

She began 2009 serenading First Lady Michelle Obama and President Barack Obama in the hours directly after the presidential inauguration in January. Then she launched into the 'I Am…' world tour, carving out time along the way to see some sights for a change. This was, too, the year when Beyoncé graciously invited Taylor Swift onstage at the MTV VMAs, to give the acceptance speech Swift had been denied by an infamous Kanye West interruption. To round off 2009, she worked right up until Christmas. While most people would be hunkering down for a round of family festivities (or bickering), Beyoncé filmed a couple of advertisements for Style Savvy, a fashion-focused Nintendo video game that she used to promote her Deréon clothing brand.

This method of working right up until the last possible moment typified 2009. But along the way, Beyoncé had allowed herself the luxury of taking in her surroundings while jetting around the world. This sparked a desire to slow down, and continue to approach travel less as a means to an end – work – and rather as an experience in itself. In a life spent rushing from one commitment to the next, typically waking at 6a.m. before finalizing a shoot or deadline at 1a.m., before hitting repeat, she craved a different pace. And so, at the start of 2010, she announced a work hiatus. She committed to spending six months away from the studio and stage. Of course, this being a Beyoncé hiatus, she wouldn't disappear entirely from the public eye, reappearing in the summer of 2010 with a video for the track 'Why Don't You Love Me?'

Overall, though, the period after the release of *I Am… Sasha Fierce* encompassed a new era for Beyoncé. By the end of 2011, she had marked out her own territory as an artist and woman, scratching out a dividing line between her early, hungry years and the more settled confidence that followed. For so long, Beyoncé had counted on the support of bandmates, and then her nuclear family. Nearing thirty, and hurtling towards the time at which the 'young' would be knocked off the front of her womanhood, she knew she had some hard decisions to make. She would have to trust herself, in ways in which she had not yet been allowed. She would, finally, need to step out from under the protective wing of her father.

* * * * *

With rebirth came a death. Devoid of much fanfare, Beyoncé retired her Sasha Fierce alter ego in early 2010. For a good few years by that point, the public – beyond just the most devout fans – had wrapped their heads around the idea of a split in Beyoncé's personality. You had the 'regular' Beyoncé, the shy Southern woman who'd always struggled to make new friends. Then, of course, you had the 'on' Beyoncé, a lightning bolt of a performer, an immutable force onstage.

In 2008, Beyoncé had talked an *Oprah Winfrey Show* audience through the step-by-step process needed to summon Sasha. The alter ego would begin to take over 'usually when I hear the crowd, when I put on my stilettos', and a sense of nervousness began to flood through her body. 'Then Sasha Fierce appears in my posture, and the way I speak and everything is different,' she said. Winfrey deftly guided Beyoncé towards verbalizing this process, the star closing the interview by sharing the simple summation that Sasha was 'kind of this character that I've created over the years' who shows up 'whenever I have to perform'.

By her hiatus year, the need for Sasha Fierce had ebbed away, exposing a realization: deferring to a stage persona was only tying complicated knots in Beyoncé's understanding of herself. Speaking to *Allure* magazine in 2010, she said her alter ego was dead. 'I don't need Sasha Fierce anymore, because I've grown, and I'm now able to merge the two,' she said. 'I want people to see me. I want people to see who I am.' This reads as a basic enough statement – perhaps even one verging on the fringes of platitude. But within the context of Beyoncé's experience, this merging of personalities divides two major sections of her career. Ever since her childhood, Beyoncé had learned to separate her performer self from her 'real' self. She had, as mentioned, led something of a double life in school, keeping her pageants and talent shows a secret from her classmates.

Coming into the 2010s, though, a life transition clicked into gear. Years spent flicking back and forth between Beyoncé Knowles the person and Beyoncé the star had started to blur into a mess. It would be easier, instead, to reconcile the two. Sasha Fierce had turned into a receptacle for Beyoncé's less palatable traits: fury, passion, sexuality often misunderstood as vulgarity, self-assuredness bordering on the cocky. In an industry that still struggled to accept women artists as thoughtful, sensual, flawed and caring all at once, retiring Sasha Fierce granted Beyoncé a certain freedom.

She was finally able to admit that there were parts of her personality that may alienate people. If some fans only wanted a smiley, bouncy singer who never shouted or demanded more from those working with her, they would be in for a shock as Beyoncé matured. If some fans were only interested in a performer telling love stories over pop beats, they too would have to come to terms with a change. At this point in her life, Beyoncé started to sit back more comfortably in her Blackness, initially via the music itself. Soon, a vocal pro-Blackness would extend to her visual work, and later to the more publicly known examples of her advocacy projects. First, though, she would make her most authentically R&B and soul album to date. *4*, named after her favourite number, ushered in a major reset.

* * * * *

Beyoncé was underwater. During her work hiatus, she plunged into the Red Sea, on a scuba-diving expedition. She ended up finding something in the depths that she hadn't expected: a sense of clarity. While guiding herself through the warm, crystalline water, the huge blooms of coral reefs captivated the star's attention. 'I was in such a great, peaceful state,' she later said, 'it inspired purity.' She would distil that purity into her next album, and the ethos that guided it.

4 was unlike anything the world had heard from Beyoncé before. In 2011, few critics would have coupled her name with experimentalism. (And perhaps that was their loss.) Sequestered away, she had thrust herself into her most ambitious album to date. At least 60 songs were written, recorded and produced, of which only 12 made the cut. Beyoncé spent so much time in the studio because she was finally able to play. Rather than pushing through studio sessions, hunting for the next hit, the process behind *4* took a winding, exploratory turn. 'I wanted this record to come from a raw place,' Beyoncé said, speaking to *W* magazine in 2011. 'Playing Etta James in the movie *Cadillac Records* really changed me. It was a darker character, and I realized that if anything is too comfortable, I want to run from it. It's no fun being safe.' In a separate interview she also noted that James gave her a 'better understanding of who I am', which she channelled into her music to come.

Running from comfort, though, meant yanking from a distinctly un-pop pile of influences. At first, Nigerian afrobeat legend Fela Kuti inspired a batch of recordings for *4*. She went so far as to work with the band from the biographical Broadway musical *Fela!*, to peer closer at the rhythms and tones that set her heart alight. 'What I learned most from Fela was artistic freedom: he just felt the spirit,' she said, speaking to *Billboard* in 2011. Of course, *4* did not become a tribute album to afrobeat. But she carried her appreciation of the abandon of African rhythms into her writing elsewhere, and developed an open-hearted approach to the album overall.

It would come to encapsulate seventies and nineties R&B, smothered in her rawest studio vocals so far. But between classic R&B came flourishes of soul, rock even, and a return to horns. Nothing sounded predictable, and few songs matched the texture of chart-toppers at the time. This was, indeed, the peak of fist-thumping, high-pitched dance music aligning with pop, creating dancefloor-fillers by Rihanna and Calvin Harris, David Guetta and Black Eyed Peas. Beyoncé could have put together an album of hits along those lines, without much problem. It may well have been what some expected.

Instead, she took the lessons of her sabbatical to heart. She had travelled extensively, visiting Egypt, traversing the Great Wall of China, enjoying the languid, 'regular' pace of picking her nephew Julez up from school or riding on a theme-park rollercoaster with him and her husband. Slowing the pace of her life in this way made Beyoncé reassess the purpose of an album. Yes, it certainly could be a showcase for singles – but an album could also, however, be a body of work. A time capsule to which Beyoncé could always return, knowing 'this is how I felt in 2010 and 2011'. And that's what she did with 4. 'Right now, this part of my life is all about embracing change and going to the next level, taking risks and showing my bravery,' she said to *Dazed & Confused* magazine in 2011. 'Not being safe. Not doing the song that everyone else on pop radio sounds like.' She had realized that she didn't have to follow the herd. 'I feel like I've earned that right. Risks excite me.'

2011 saw her undertake one of her biggest career risks, in a different sense. In March, before the summer release of 4, Beyoncé went public with the news that she was terminating her professional relationship with her father, Mathew Knowles. 'I've only parted ways with my father on a business level', read the statement put out by Parkwood Entertainment (Beyoncé's own management company, founded in 2008; see Chapter X). Mathew's statement followed the very next day, adding that 'business is business and family is family', before reciprocating an expression of love that Beyoncé had made in her statement.

Behind the scenes, possible reasons for the split had rumbled for some time. For one, Mathew Knowles fathered a child outside of his marriage to Tina, which ultimately led her to file for divorce in December 2009. Beyoncé had also been told that her father might have been siphoning funds away from her profits and in October 2010 she hired a legal team to conduct an audit. The results were inconclusive, and he filed a suit against Beyoncé's tour promoters Live Nation, believing they had poisoned his daughter against him. A judge eventually sided with Live Nation.

Legal wrangling aside, Beyoncé emerged from this tumultuous time stronger than ever. She elected to manage herself and set about hiring a team to drive every division of Parkwood Entertainment. It would soon become the crux of her working life. And after about 20 years, she no longer employed either of her parents. That little Houston girl was setting out on her own, after inching from one incremental stage of independence to the next. First, the full family affair had run her working life. Then, of course, she'd found camaraderie in her bandmates. Now, as a solo star in command of the ups and downs of her career, she was building a family and business empire.

Her partnership with Jay-Z, both intimately and creatively, formed a cornerstone of this latest leap towards professional autonomy. She was becoming her own boss, with a powerful, caring husband at her side. Within a matter of years, she would be taking care of both her career and a family of her own.

The decision to fire her father took courage. Yet, even when thinking about the music on 4, Beyoncé had reached a stage where she felt able to summon up the bravery needed to take a chance. The album's first single, 'Run the World

(Girls)', functions as a symbol for this change. Speaking to *Billboard*, she said the song, and its abrasive, tap-tap staccato beat, reminded her to take charge. 'I can never be safe; I always try and go against the grain,' she said. 'As soon as I accomplish one thing, I just set a higher goal. That's how I've gotten to where I am.'

VIII.

Through Her Eyes

On a Thursday in April 2012, Beyoncé made what would be considered an innocuous move for someone half her age. She launched a public account on blogging site Tumblr. Her announcement on beyonce.tumblr.com set out her tone and intentions from the very start. 'This is my life, today, over the years – through my eyes', read a handwritten note posted on the site, presented as beautifully as the images she would later add. 'My family, my travels, my love. This is where I share with you. This will continue to grow as I do. Love Beyoncé.'

By this point, Beyoncé was a new mother to daughter Blue Ivy Carter, born on 7 January 2012. And so, of course, joining Tumblr was a savvy and productive choice for her – more so than it would be for a typical, slightly bored fifteen-year-old at the time. Most of Beyoncé's fan inter-actions up until the early 2010s had happened in person, at gig meet-and-greets or on the special occasions where she would pay a particular fan, or group of fans, an in-person 'stunt' visit. But online, connecting with Beyoncé was, up until this time, a one-way street of fan obsession and fascination. The BeyHive sprang up on forums, dedicated websites, in the comments sections of pop-culture blogs and on social media fan accounts. With the arrival of Blue Ivy, fans were desperate to see inside the family life Beyoncé was developing. Previously on this subject, their 'queen', however, had been largely silent.

This was soon to change, and 2012 marks the first year in which Beyoncé opened up to the public, sharing images from her personal life. Of course, those images were meted out in a carefully orchestrated fashion. But her Tumblr account drafted a template that would go on to shape so much of the star's impact as an image-maker. A year later, she released self-directed 2013 documentary *Life Is But a Dream*, revealing intimate stories about her father, motherhood, her marriage, and sharing for the first time that she had lived through a miscarriage.

It's worth noting that on the very day she joined Tumblr, Beyoncé also sent out her first tweet to more than 3 million followers who had waited years to hear directly from the star. She created her Twitter account in April 2009, keeping schtum as most users chattered on, using the app in its early days almost as a public texting tool. Over time, it would become clear that visual media, rather than the 140-character written word, was her preferred mode of mass communication.

Throughout her life, Beyoncé had learned – often on the fly and on the job – how to cultivate a public persona. Thus, she had spent the majority of her life contorting in order to see herself from the perspective of millions of strangers. In her early thirties, however, she began to take charge of how she was viewed in a more meaningful way than ever. In the coming years, her creative work would marry the aural and visual, seemingly rewriting pop industry rules in the process. But first, she would have to learn how to share. And, crucially, how much.

* * * * *

Back in 2007, Beyoncé didn't bother to pretend to use social media. By her own account, she hardly went online at all. When interviewed by British actor, DJ and presenter Reggie Yates, she delicately sidestepped a question about her use of MySpace, a major social network at the time. Yates set her up gently, making what ought to have seemed a safe assumption.

'It's almost like you've got your mobile phone, you go home, you check your MySpace and then you check your email too,' he began, in an effort to paint a picture of how ubiquitous the site had become. Of course, the interview itself was sponsored by MySpace, and his slick plug was likely designed to give fans an insight into how Beyoncé was just like them – a user of the site, who curated the page on which she had racked up hordes of 'friends'.

But Yates would not get the answer he may have wanted. Beyoncé diligently nodded along, diplomatically making sure to highlight just how important the proto-social network was for 'a lot of people' in music. She quickly admitted that she never really opened the site herself. 'I'm still a little behind, and I work so hard that I don't have time to do those things,' she said. If she was at home, she would be heading towards her bed to snatch a few hours of sleep before her next commitment.

At that point in her life, Beyoncé approached image-building conventionally. She remained, principally, a glamorous entertainment figurehead, a cascade of healthy, illuminated skin and hair with high-shine outfits to match. Branching out into acting had, by 2007, largely allowed her to embody glamorous performers – the titular character in MTV's *Carmen: A Hip Hopera*; Foxxy Cleopatra in *Austin Powers*; Deena Jones (a Diana Ross facsimile) in *Dreamgirls*; and Xania from the much-maligned 2006 *Pink Panther* prequel. This image, especially in her work as a musician, came as second nature. Beyoncé's hyper-feminine styling extended deep roots into her Southern upbringing, anchored as it was by her mother, Tina. From witnessing Tina run a beauty business during her childhood, to the development of Destiny's Child's aesthetic, Beyoncé picked up on certain cues about how she ought to look, and present publicly. By the time she went solo, this branding had become a money-maker of its own and Beyoncé became a cosmetics ambassador and aspirational beauty figure for women of all ethnicities.

Throughout her early years, however, Beyoncé had deferred to her parents on most of her image decisions. In interview after interview, teenage Beyoncé and her band-mates countered questions about their 'revealing' outfits with the firm acknowledgement that a mother figure of the group had designed the clothing. On the more commercial side, her father Mathew Knowles had experimented with ways to keep Destiny's Child in the public eye. They would appear in ads for fast food, or supermarkets, or hair products marketed at Black women. In these ads, ranging from 1998 to 2005, the group would often be transplanted, fully styled, into whatever environment the treatment required. The slickly gelled ponytails, smoothly laid edges, taut expanses of midriff – all would appear as though the group were about to head straight to a video shoot.

But these adverts *felt* like ads. They lacked a connection to the girls or a sense that the group bought into whatever they were helping to sell. Before Destiny's Child announced their end in 2005, they had wandered deathly close to over-exposure. In an E! 2002 special on the group, just as they cemented their three-person line-up, then-editor-in-chief of *Vibe* magazine Emil Wilbekin had said as much. 'Everywhere you looked, there was Destiny's Child,' he said. 'They're in the Target ad, they're preparing their Christmas album, they're going to be at the All-Star Game' – it felt, as he put it, 'too much'. By the mid-2000s, fans knew of Beyoncé through her music, press interviews and via the unfortunate 'drama' of her group's line-up change. But she had not been in charge. She had not yet grabbed the reins and controlled how the public was to view her. That would come in the first few years in which she finally managed herself. It was her decision to make, and ultimately hers alone.

* * * * *

It only took a couple of years for everything to change. Beyoncé had started the 2010s maintaining her warm, polite-yet-guarded public demeanour. She would only really share details of her life in more traditional interview formats, whether broadcast or print. More often than not, those carefully constructed narratives focused on her work, rather than her private life. A private life was private for a reason, after all. Yet, by 2012, her initial reticence to open up online had surged into a strategy overhaul. By the end of that year, she had added an Instagram account to her social media repertoire. And this, a visual medium, would become the arena in which she would dominate.

Coupling a presence on Tumblr with a heavily customized Instagram account (not to mention a Facebook page that blended promotional material with behind-the-scenes content), Beyoncé soon settled on a rhythm and style of image-making. It not only cemented her place as a one-of-a-kind celebrity on social media but went on to inspire later trends and digital platforms.

For one, Beyoncé continued to use Tumblr regularly for several years. Between 2012 and late 2016, she posted frequent photo-only updates to the site. Of course, Tumblr is home to countless forms of sharing, from long text posts and combative conversations to the borderline pornography that was largely wiped from the site following its Verizon acquisition in 2017. In short: if you had just about anything to share with strangers on the internet, you could do it on Tumblr.

In Beyoncé's case, that entailed a visual diary. Simple, single-photo posts that practically filled a laptop screen. More specifically, hers were the sort of diary entries you would make if you knew that millions of people would be on the lookout for your innermost thoughts. As a result, her Tumblr account felt both intimate and tightly controlled. To fans, it offered never-before-seen images of their idol, curled up on a couch make-up free, or stepping out of a short-term rental property before attending Coachella festival in 2015.

In this sweet spot of time before Instagram morphed into the loudest voice in visual sharing, Beyoncé crafted her Tumblr page with a curatorial and all-seeing eye.

There was more to the strategy than beyonce.tumblr. com. As a second point, Beyoncé elevated 'one-off' Tumblr accounts into entire publicity moments. She and her husband, Jay-Z, opened a now-defunct account at helloblueivycarter. tumblr.com, in February 2012. With it, they shared the first public images of Blue Ivy, almost a month after her birth. So much for linking arms with a celebrity print magazine such as *People* or *OK!*, and granting them the exclusive right to publish the introductory photos. What was it, 2007? No – by 2012, Beyoncé was firmly shaping her own narrative. Self-publishing offered a level of control that no amount of money for exclusivity could buy.

Finally, Beyoncé's very aesthetic became a brand of its own. As she grew up in the public eye, so too did her sense of style and how she chose to express it. Unlike the staged posters and promotional shoots of her teen years, her social media imagery crackles with the lo-fi 'noise' of film photography, or pops with a stark flash that you can imagine bursting from a bulb. The lo-fi images look more candid, while she tends to be posed for those lit with the bright flash. In either case, you're offered a glance behind the velvet rope, at how Beyoncé may primp and pose before an event, or how she'll mean-mug with a faux snarl between takes while on set during a video shoot.

For such a private star, this has proven a masterful strategy. Beyoncé is a rare celebrity who does not need to pair Instagram photos with captions. Fans don't expect her to explain herself or offer up a clever pun. Former head of digital at Parkwood, Lauren Wirtzer-Seawood, summed Instagram up as a 'personal communications tool' for her boss, in 2014. 'We're very careful not to be too salesy in anything that we do,' she said, at that year's Web Summit conference. 'That's not the kind of relationship that Beyoncé has with her fans. She wants it to be organic, and she wants it to really come from her. And it does.'

That honesty shows. Though critics largely panned *Life Is But a Dream*, the film's seeming obsession with fame and its subject's relation to celebrity carries a salience to this day. At the time, her focus on herself seemed overblown, a sort of ridiculous exercise in puffery. But seen through the lens of a pervasive 'selfie culture' that would follow, her hours of footage – some self-filmed on laptops and phones, others collected by her staff – resemble the typical smartphone camera roll of anyone born after 1985.

What might have appeared self-conscious or contrived in 2013 now looks like an average Instagram story, whether uploaded by a close friend or an influencer. Fans have gone so far as to joke that her music video for single '7/11' – filmed on a mobile phone, in a hotel suite – essentially created TikTok before TikTok. The video-sharing platform does share an undeniably similar aesthetic with the '7/11' visuals; both trade in a self-aware playfulness. Jokes aside, she has maintained a vision that manages to stay a few steps ahead of the herd, even though she is resolutely a mainstream, pop figure.

Her branding extended offline, too. In 2011, she had partnered with Michelle Obama on public health childhood obesity campaign Let's Move! – accompanied by a dance-workout video filmed in a school cafeteria. She donated her $4 million *Cadillac Records* paycheque to Phoenix House, a rehab centre that invited her in to hear from those living with addiction, up-close. And setting up BeyGood formally in 2013 lent a visual, digital signature to this work too. Hashtagging its name signalled to fans: 'this is something I care about – I want you to join me'.

2013 would become a pivotal year in the making of Beyoncé, the superstar. But already, her potency as a visual thinker was mushrooming, taking shape. Weaving images and sound into her work would become something of a calling card. And, truly, no one was quite ready for her.

IX.

Secrets, Surprises

Surprises are funny old things. Done right, they're delightful. When they don't land, their glimpse into the unknown can translate into horror. But when Beyoncé flings work into the world unannounced, she inspires a reaction more akin to hysteria.

Her self-titled fifth studio album emerged in a digital format, initially available only on iTunes. It materialized, without any of the usual promotional fanfare, on 13 December 2013, and the release exploded into an event in itself. But listeners were then confronted with an album miles away from the norm. From its rollout to its delivery, *Beyoncé* staked out new ground. And it did so not just for Beyoncé as an artist, but the broader pop music industry.

By sharing the album simultaneously with both press and public, Beyoncé reached over the aisle to engage her fans without reviewers, radio play or even a promotional video serving as intermediaries. She thus entered yet another chapter in her career. Discussing Beyoncé can quickly lead to hyperbole, but it's no exaggeration to label this as the time when she became a game-changer. She was by no means the first artist to toy with radical release strategies. Yet the way in which she pulled the entertainment world into her orbit, for one day in December, came to underpin both her thinking and her impact in the years to come.

To be a game-changer, of course, implies playing the game. For all Beyoncé's accomplishments at this time, she still kept a close eye on her public image, allowing the mask to slip only once – to near-devastating effect – in an elevator in 2014. There is, though, a lot to be gleaned from her perspective as a woman, barely into her thirties, who was well on her way to pop-culture monolith status. This was the beginning of Beyoncé: living icon.

* * * * *

Let's start with the numbers. *Beyoncé* ballooned quickly into a commercial success. It became her fifth consecutive album to debut at the top of the Billboard Hot 200 chart, downloaded 430,000 times on its release day on iTunes. The album sold 1.3 million copies in the US in its first 17 days out, which was enough to place it in the ten best-selling worldwide albums of 2013, despite there being only a fortnight before the year's end.

It's easy for '17 days of sales' not to mean much. So this may help: it was, according to Apple, the fastest-selling album in iTunes history at that point. A cool 828,773 downloads bestowed upon it that honour, and it sped to the top of the iTunes album charts in 104 countries. The album eventually went double platinum in the UK, and platinum in both Australia and New Zealand. It went to number 1 in Canada, too. More aptly for a 2010s release, the album inspired more than 1.2 million tweets in its first 12 hours in the public sphere.

But the album was more than a collection of recordings as 17 music videos accompanied the 14 songs. OK, those are more numbers, but their prominence belies a sucker punch of creative heft. This wasn't just mellifluous pop music rendered lifelike by a couple of music videos. With *Beyoncé*, the singer whipped up an aural-visual body of work that demanded repeat viewings, and then repeat listens. You felt that if you blinked too long, you might miss some other sumptuous detail. And so, to catch every reference or coded meaning, you would hit pause, rewind, play, again and again. By the time the album hit other music streaming services besides iTunes, you could home in on just the music, on luscious production. Leaping from disco to trap to hand-clap, fireside singalongs, *Beyoncé* deployed an arsenal of entirely unpredictable sounds and collaborators.

Next: the process. As one might by now expect, *Beyoncé* started as a bulging collection of about 80 songs. The album pushed forward both the presentation and construction of two of its predecessors, *B'Day* and *4*. For one, Beyoncé had, in essence, already made a visual album before her 'first' visual album in 2013, by creating a video for every song on *B'Day* – a fact not often noted. The *B'Day* videos were less ambitious than the cinematic, erotic and sometimes dream-like *Beyoncé* crop. But they showed that even under her father's watchful eye at the time, Beyoncé was experimenting with the album form.

She worked with several producers and songwriters on *B'Day*, and on *4*, she maintained that 'hit factory' approach, bringing in a broad range of producers over whose beats she sang. Whereas *B'Day* was recorded in about two weeks

(Beyoncé booked out Sony's entire recording studio facility in New York City), she worked on *4* for the best part of a year. She needed that time to bridge the gap between her Mathew Knowles years and her self-management to follow. Similarly, *Beyoncé* was recorded over about a year and a half – the time Beyoncé needed to pick up the pop industry norms, shake them furiously and then upend them entirely.

And so, finally, to the album's release. In this respect, *Beyoncé*'s influence on pop music ought not to be understated. She coupled a Destiny's Child-era habit – working with a truckload of producers – with a sharp curatorial ear and an as-yet revolutionary release plan. As media analyst Mark Mulligan put it in 2013, 'Think about the decades of A&R practice that kind of got thrown out the window! I'm hard-pressed to find a precedent for it.'

Sounding not unlike a culture commentator herself, Beyoncé condensed the internet's imploding impact on music marketing into a few brief sentences. 'Now people only listen to a few seconds of a song… and they don't really invest in the whole experience. It's all about the single, and the hype,' she said in 2013. 'I just want this to come out when it's ready and from me to my fans.' In practice, that meant doing everything she could to avoid 'leaks', when whole, unfinished songs could easily end up floating around online before they were ready.

And so *Beyoncé* was kept under close surveillance, code-named 'Lily' and only discussed by select Parkwood and Sony staff, and a few key people at Apple. Even the dancers cast in the videos were only given need-to-know information. They had only vague ideas about why they were memorizing body-contorting choreography, shooting some videos as late as September before the album's December release.

'The whole process was very secretive,' James Krausse, who helped mix the album, recalled in 2018. 'The only person I told was my wife.' Teresa LaBarbera Whites, Beyoncé's A&R (who you may recall helped sign Beyoncé as a teenager), backed this up, too: 'Only a handful of us knew what was actually happening and when it was happening.'

In the years since, the 'surprise drop' has become a cultural tool in music, sometimes wielded like a sledge-hammer, or given as a delicate gift thrust into the arms of fans at others. Artists ranging from Eminem, Drake and 21 Savage to multi-genre experimenter (and sibling) Solange have followed Beyoncé's lead in releasing albums without any advance notice.

Others, from pop star Taylor Swift, alternative stalwarts Radiohead (pioneers of the form in 2007) and Björk, soul-funk hybrid D'Angelo and Kanye West, have granted fans some, often brief advance notice before sudden releases. But they forewent the usual rigamarole of radio singles, music videos and so on. As if to say, 'go on, there's the album – have at it.'

As a star of her stature, Beyoncé was feeling her way through an unknown: the sensation of taking control, without knowing what may unfold. That created a natural tension. For so long, she had been trained, preened, inspired, all for greater commercial success under her father's tutelage. Now, those metrics for success were cast aside with his expired manager status. So what did it mean to be good? What had all her hard work been for? She drilled into that question on *Beyoncé*, ultimately making an album that may not have produced a smash hit single. But the stories she told, the detail with which she divulged her thoughts on sexual pleasure, marriage, femininity and feminism, delivered value. 'My message behind this album was finding the beauty in imperfection,' she said.

Looking back on the little girl who had smiled wider and sung louder in beauty pageants and talent shows, she considered the childhood she had missed. In the video for the song 'Pretty Hurts', she confronts those past cups and rosettes. 'The trophy represents all of the sacrifices I made as a kid,' she said. 'All of the time that I lost being on the road, in the studios, as a child. And I just want to blow that shit up,' she laughed.

By early 2014, Beyoncé was ready to accept what happens when you blow up your own frame of reference. She ran towards imperfection, rather than recoiling from it. At the same time, her infallibility was almost a persona in its own right – the most common iteration of her name becoming 'Queen Bey'. Within months, though, she would – in a rare instance – stand exposed in front of millions, minus her usual control.

* * * * *

At the Met Gala of 2014, Beyoncé looked beautiful. Draped in Givenchy haute couture, she smouldered from behind a bejewelled veil. Her deep, beaded neckline and sheer dress sparkled correspondingly. Some of these embellishments jutted out, looking like tiny hand-sewn spikes. And while she gracefully made her way onto most 'best-dressed' lists of the major annual fashion event, her red carpet arrival was later to be upstaged.

Just a week later millions would swarm search engines, desperate to find what has become known as the 'elevator incident'. Grainy surveillance footage captured in a hotel elevator showed Beyoncé's sister, Solange, thrashing at Jay-Z, held back from landing more blows by a bodyguard. Beyoncé mostly stood with her arms by her sides, hardly engaging.

The trio was leaving a Met Gala afterparty in New York. Outside, paparazzi sent blinding camera flashes into the night air. The employee who had slipped the footage to gossip site TMZ was fired within days, but not before reportedly exchanging the video for $250,000. TMZ happily refer to it as one of their top-five most popular scoops of all time. And to this day, neither Beyoncé, Solange or Jay-Z has publicly explained why the fight exploded.

'There has been a great deal of speculation about what triggered the unfortunate incident', all three said, in a joint statement at the time. 'But the most important thing is that our family has worked through it.' This acknowledgement, with no further detail, pulled Beyoncé back from the brink of a PR disaster. Although much was made of the video at the time, the bulk of feverish speculation buzzed around her sister, with people diagnosing Solange from afar (her family denied intoxication or mental health issues were at play) or openly mocking her. Somehow, Beyoncé came out on the other side of summer 2014 without a mark.

This is because she said nothing at all. Consider how the 'elevator incident' panned out compared to LaTavia

Roberson and LeToya Luckett's departure from Destiny's Child. Back then, Beyoncé had been wheeled out repeatedly to face the press; taking a sort of 'tackle this head-on' approach, which ended up dredging the story back up as journalists reacted to every slight development. Beyoncé and Kelly Rowland looked visibly annoyed then, rattled by their obligation to thrust this private moment into the spotlight.

Just months after her industry-defining fifth album, Beyoncé would not roll up her sleeves and dive into the muck. Her silence then became something of a media theme. In time, her power was such that she would be granted glossy magazine covers without being interviewed by a journalist: famously, for a September issue of American *Vogue*.

At other times, she recorded interviews for her own archive, as journalists recorded her. She was nowhere near the younger woman who had done the rounds, talking on drive-time radio or late-night chat shows. Increasingly, she would only speak on her own terms. For journalists accustomed to plenty of 'access' – i.e., hours spent in the company of their celebrity interview subjects – this subtle change hit like a slap. But it was another manifestation of Beyoncé's specific kind of control. That word comes up often, only because it encompasses so much of her solo career, from about her third album onwards. By this stage, she had begun to reckon with her mind-boggling level of celebrity. Retaining a haven of both privacy and control helped her cling on to a sense of self. Without it, how many of us would survive the scrutiny that she constantly endured?

In December, she shared a short film, marking the first anniversary of her self-titled album's dramatic entrance.

It plays like a meditation, a baring of her inner thoughts. 'I was brought up seeing my mother trying to please and make everyone comfortable,' she said at one point. 'I always felt like it was my job to fix the problem. People-pleaser.' As she grew up, she said she came to shed that deferential demeanour. Not wanting to please others also translated to seeking less outside validation.

A case in point: the Grammy awards in January 2015. By most accounts, Beyoncé had shattered the expectations set for her, as a pop star. Her self-titled album had veered off the well-trodden path for major label releases, hacking through a thicket of unknowns. And she had emerged on the other side with a commercial triumph and armfuls of critical praise. Though it had had a commercial success many recording artists would envy, *Beyoncé* was never going to be her biggest-selling album. It had sold 5 million copies globally between 2013 and 2016. Comparatively, according to Sony, her solo debut *Dangerously in Love* sold about 11 million copies worldwide between 2003 and 2007. *Beyoncé*'s impact, though, reset the dial for pop music, ever so subtly. It sounded like nothing else being made by another singer on a par with her celebrity status.

Walking into the 57th annual Grammy awards show, you might have figured she was a shoo-in for that coveted Album of the Year statuette. Instead, that year's prize went to alternative-rock act Beck, for his album *Morning Phase*. Don't be fooled – Beyoncé still ended the night with three awards, taking her total Grammys tally to 20. Still, there was an overarching sense that she had been snubbed. Notably, she was only awarded in genre categories coded as Black. Her

R&B Performance and R&B Song nominations for 'Drunk in Love' yielded wins. But outside this somewhat narrow framing, she also picked up an award for Best Surround Sound Album (formerly Best Immersive Sound).

In her 15 years in the spotlight, she had often been pigeonholed by major awards in this way. Funnily enough, that tended to happen even when her music sounded its most 'pop', with her Blackness nudged to the edge of her fans' vision. In just a couple of years, the content of her music would evolve once again. Whether the voting Recording Academy members kept up would be anyone's guess. Call it another surprise if you wish.

X.

Beyoncé Inc.

Parkwood Entertainment changed Beyoncé's career – and life – for good. And for the better, too. The business truly came into its own during the making and rollout of *Beyoncé*. But Beyoncé had been building it up for years. Since founding Parkwood in her twenties, its purpose grew more clearly defined, its ambitions reaching further towards the sky.

In not much more than a decade, the company morphed through several iterations. Primarily, it began as a video and film production unit. Feature films *Cadillac Records* (2008) and *Obsessed* (2009) fell under its initial purview – although both films were made in collaboration with other production houses. Within a decade, though, Parkwood's remit would span artist management, TV, apparel, philanthropy, a record label and select outside investments.

Beyoncé opting to manage her career and dismiss her father firmly jammed Parkwood Entertainment's flag in the fresh earth of her future. 'When I decided to manage myself, it was important that I didn't go to some big management company,' she said in 2013. 'I felt like I wanted to follow the footsteps of Madonna and be a powerhouse and have my own empire and show other women when you get to this point in your career you don't have to go sign with someone else and share your money and your success.' Instead, as she summarized, you get it done yourself.

At first, Beyoncé had only meant for the company to be a video production arm. Instead, at various stages throughout her solo career, Parkwood – named after a Houston street on which the Knowles family once lived – would reinforce her sense of independence. It granted her multiple streams of creative expression – a rarity for a musician in her position, expected to cede much control to the fame game. Tightly controlling the company's inner workings allowed her to find a space of her own in the fishbowl of celebrity. She was able to live in some ways like an independent artist, while signed to one of the 'big three' major labels. To understand her progression in her thirties, you have to understand Beyoncé Inc.

* * * * *

After moving Parkwood's headquarters from Houston to a Manhattan office in 2011, Beyoncé sketched out her rise from performer to chairwoman. Just a couple of years into running her business, she reflected on the notion of ownership. 'Now I'm controlling my content, controlling my brand and archiving it for my daughter,' she began. 'You see Puffy [rapper and entrepreneur Sean Combs], and you see my husband and you see these male artists that become moguls, and the female artists might become legends, but there's not enough of us that become moguls.' This concept, of trying to own the means of production rather than solely turn up and perform, would nudge her along. The goal: mogul status.

To achieve it, she brought on a team of assistants, executives and digital media experts who helped her redefine her place in pop culture. Her publicist, Yvette Noel-Schure, and A&R lead, Teresa LaBarbera Whites, had been with Beyoncé (and Destiny's Child) from the very beginning. She slotted them into prominent roles at Parkwood. She also brought in visual director Ed Burke – often marvelled at by journalists as the person solely responsible for filming and documenting hours of her life. Creative directors, a general manager, a brand manager; all found themselves among the core group that would come to delight fans and fascinate many a music business commentator.

You can demarcate this as a time when Beyoncé transitioned from a symbol, or product in the marketplace, to the distributor of a variety of ideas and investments. At this time, many other Black American musicians were toying with novel ways to express themselves. It couldn't all be writing, recording, promoting, touring, in an infinite loop. No – artists from rappers Tyler, The Creator and Donald Glover to funk genre-bender Janelle Monáe also spent the 2010s pushing back against the constraints of what a musician was expected to do. They successfully dipped into designing apparel, programming festivals, acting, nurturing other artists on labels or collectives. Through Parkwood, Beyoncé often appeared the most visible in these efforts, but her venture into a diversified creative output swam shoulder to shoulder against the tide with other Black artists. This change had been decades in the making.

The music industry had historically done the bare minimum to support Black American acts, siloing them off in racially segregated charts, venues and radio stations since the advent of recorded music. Fundamentally, white record label executives invested very little in so-called 'race records' between the 1920s and 1940s. Record labels belatedly clocked the appeal of Black American blues, a thundering hotbed of lyrical heft. And yet Black performers were offered terrible deals.

Some would be persuaded to record original songs without so much as a signed contract, while others inadvertently agreed to deeply exploitative terms as performers. In the 1920s, Blues pioneer Bessie Smith famously earned no royalties while making Columbia Records millions as the first Black woman whose recordings they pressed. In time, Black artists would find their songs handed to white counterparts to be repackaged for 'mainstream' – read white – audiences. The minds behind many major 1950s and 1960s hits would not earn royalties for their work.

Sure, by the early 2000s, terms weren't as brutally unfair. But the music industry had still not been substantially overhauled – incremental change had bred progress, rather than a complete rethinking of the relationships between Black creators and record labels. Prince tugged at the confines of the label-to-artist relationship for years. And just ask groups such as TLC or NWA about the complexity of contractual pitfalls.

Beyoncé emerged into adulthood in the shadow of that history. By the 2010s, Parkwood offered her the chance to forge a sense of independence, even as one of the most famous women in entertainment. Further forays into apparel, film and philanthropy facilitated this independence.

From one project to the next, she was showing that she had more to offer the world than performing – of course, her contributions in that realm were already near-stratospheric. In 2014, she established the Ivy Park clothing line – named after her daughter and her childhood neighbourhood's Parkwood Park. The brand began as a joint venture with fast-fashion retailer Topshop, picking up where the middling success of House of Deréon (in collaboration with her mother) had left off.

This time, Beyoncé drove aspirational messaging into the core of the brand. Ivy Park's athleisure wear – mostly leggings, hoodies, bra tops, all items soft to the touch and humming with latent femininity – was perceived by fans as a route to empowerment. By its March 2016 launch, her followers were ready to receive its blend of approachable and tough styling. That overarching sense of the brand's value system was amplified when, in 2018, Beyoncé bought Topshop owner Philip Green out from the Ivy Park partnership. Green had been accused of sexual, physical and racist abuse by former staff, allegations he has firmly denied. Soon, in April 2019, she scooped up an Ivy Park deal with Adidas instead.

Ivy Park was unlike her previous endorsement deals with, say, Pepsi or L'Oréal. Her former general manager Lee Anne Callahan-Longo described the joint venture in 2015 as a clear evolution. Beyoncé was now, to be blunt, famous enough to be choosy. 'So we decided that endorsements were not something that she was interested in anymore,' Callahan-Longo said. 'You know, "why am I using my face, my brand, my voice to sell someone else's products?

I'd rather invest in me.'" This is why you no longer see Beyoncé's smiling face in adverts for another company's product. She has leveraged herself in a way that is still, at least within pop music, rare.

This is because she cares deeply. When her name is attached to a project or a piece of work, Beyoncé is the sort of perfectionist who can't resist then checking over people's shoulders to make sure everything is in line with her vision. Awe tends to surround her commitment to every element of her work in this way. Footage taken at various points in her career will show her checking the lighting before one show, firmly tweaking the choreography before another. This attention to detail then extended to how she approached film.

Where *Cadillac Records* had flopped at the box office, *Obsessed* made millions but was critically panned. So Parkwood pivoted away from scripted films. Instead, it became the driving force behind music-based works, either about the process behind some of Beyoncé's later albums, or taking on the form of the albums themselves. Running her own production company allowed Beyoncé to not only surprise-release her self-titled album, but also follow its release with a package of YouTube videos delving into the making of said album. These were DVD extra features rejigged for the digital age, created and shared by the artist herself.

Her fifth album, *Lemonade*, released in partnership with HBO in 2016, would be a multimedia, audiovisual artwork. Its release became a global event, with fans around the world clamouring to attend viewing parties, or gathering around a single mobile phone streaming the film in the early hours of the morning. The hour-long film became appointment television. The music itself was teased with little promotion beyond the single 'Formation', and initially only available to stream on artist-owned service Tidal. Beyoncé once again created the mix of media circus, exclusivity and fan frenzy that had characterized *Beyoncé*'s surprise release.

Ultimately, Beyoncé learned to trust herself. She rounded out her extended pursuits with philanthropy – under the BeyGood banner – and the mentorship of young musicians, via Parkwood's record label. Primed to focus on charity through her church and family, BeyGood was founded in 2013 to align and amplify these benevolent projects. The organization could move from acquiring school supplies for children in underfunded communities to supporting those devastated by the long-running lack of clean, safe water in Flint, Michigan. In many of these projects, she cradles an implicit nurturing of Black and under-represented communities. Whether in Haiti or Houston, she threads a consistent ethos through the work. In this way, Beyoncé can advocate for oft-ignored groups and indirectly raise the question of why elected officials are not doing so. Put simply, BeyGood strives to ask: where is the accountability?

* * * * *

June 2017. Beyoncé had her hands full, looking after newborn twins, Sir and Rumi Carter, with her husband, Jay-Z. That year's BET Awards had just honoured her with the Viewers' Choice gong for *Lemonade* song 'Sorry'. Beyoncé herself was not in attendance at the live awards ceremony, having so recently given birth. Instead, two young women picked up the award on her behalf. Chloe and Halle Bailey, a sibling duo, headed onto the stage looking confident and delighted. Chloe was weeks away from her nineteenth birthday; her younger sister, Halle, was seventeen. They read a statement from Beyoncé that included a warm farewell: 'To everyone at the show tonight, you all look so beautiful, and at home, thank you and have a wonderful, wonderful night. From Beyoncé.' The Bailey sisters stood beaming onstage, in lieu of one of the world's biggest stars, because she had added them to the Parkwood Entertainment stable in 2015. By 2020, Chloe x Halle had earned Grammy nominations, acting roles on sitcom *Grown-ish* and released two studio albums. As a curator of talent, Beyoncé had found yet another skill set.

No doubt Beyoncé recognized her younger self, watching the girls perform song covers on YouTube (as many a singer is now discovered, from Canadians Justin Bieber and Alessia Cara to Australian Troye Sivan). She saw enough potential to sign the duo. And so, by expanding Parkwood into both a record label and an artist management firm, she leveraged her magic touch as a form of mentorship. Not every Parkwood artist has been as successful as Chloe x Halle, with their tight harmonies, experimental styling aesthetic and authentic pop-R&B; Sophie Beem and Ingrid Burley, for example, are as yet barely known outside the BeyHive.

Pop stars are rarely expected to be businesspeople, too. Yet Beyoncé enforces her performance prowess with the seemingly mundane decisions she makes to turn the cogs behind her star power. She watched her father closely, learning what to do – and crucially, what not to – from his manoeuvres as she grew up. Speaking in a pre-recorded message for all those graduating in 2020, she laid out the significance of her work offstage. 'The entertainment business is still very sexist. It's still very male-dominated,' she said. 'And as a woman, I did not see enough female role models given the opportunity to do what I knew I had to do, to run my label and management company, to direct my films and produce my tours. That meant ownership, owning my masters, owning my art, owning my future and writing my own story.'

Next, she was blunt on where race and gender create a suffocating Venn diagram within the industry. 'Not enough Black women had a seat at the table. So I had to go and chop down that wood and build my own table,' she said. By this, she meant building the team at Parkwood that would see her through, and which she shook up with new faces in 2016. She learned not to follow the template set at other companies, instead 'hiring women, men, outsiders, underdogs, people that were overlooked and waiting to be seen'.

In the sleek, private LA offices where her team decides how next to astound fans, she has created an incubator of talent across multimedia platforms. In the final years of the 2010s, Parkwood would propel her creative vision into a stratosphere that even she may have never imagined. At her most raw and honest, her complete arsenal of sound, visuals, live performance and curation reached a fever pitch. She was ready for her homecoming.

XI.

Black Is Legacy

At last, she floated free. Beyoncé's elaborate visual album of 2016, *Lemonade*, saw her plunged fully clothed into water, lying on her side on the grass in the New Orleans Superdome stadium, seeking answers to questions of generational betrayal. She was, for the first time, exploring her Black – and particularly Black Southern – lineage. And she did so with a focus on infidelity, forgiveness, family and the lasting impact of slavery on Black women. This album undoubtedly made the most resounding statement of her work to date. Politically, personally and visually, *Lemonade* created its own lane.

If that sounds rather heavy for an assessment of a pop album, you may want to give *Lemonade* a closer look. In one respect, it was a curatorial display that some might have expected from Beyoncé at this stage in her career – flowing dresses, sweeping shots over a Louisiana bayou and then the sudden crash of a baseball bat swung through a car window. It could simply have been considered a follow-up to the feast of videos accompanying previous album *Beyoncé*. Yet in another sense, *Lemonade* presented Beyoncé at her most vulnerable. All of those pretty visual touches served a larger point.

Really, from the early 2010s, Beyoncé was starting to square her upbringing – politically conscious parents and their pro-Black teachings, a strong maternal figure – with the role people thought she fulfilled in public. Her apolitical love songs and party floor-fillers may have, over the years, given the impression that she was a sort of pop everywoman. Or her performance flair might have suggested that her place in the world was nailed to the stage, with a role to entertain, smile, give back to charity now and then, and do little else. But this wasn't to be.

From her first pro-Obama Instagram post to the release of 2020's *Lion King* accompaniment film, *Black Is King*, she staked out a return to her roots. Regardless of what white American and international fans may have believed, Beyoncé is undeniably pro-Black. She has used her art, social media feeds and philanthropic work to identify as a feminist and explore the rich complexity of Black American life. The singer would never claim to speak on behalf of all Black Americans. And in her work she often looked to the African diaspora for both inspiration and collaborative strength, too. But by her mid-thirties, Beyoncé had earned an incomparable position of influence. She was ready to speak out for the culture.

* * * * *

The release of *Lemonade*, like *Beyoncé*, became an event. In February 2016 the singer teasingly dropped the video for the album's only single, 'Formation'. You can sum it up as: an expression of Black pride and history; a four-minute exploration of New Orleans sinking after the horror of Hurricane Katrina; a plea to the police to 'stop killing us'.

Beyoncé had hand-picked director Melina Matsoukas to make the taut, declarative video for 'Formation'. She then drew Matsoukas into working on *Lemonade* more broadly. Matsoukas, speaking in 2017, remembered that Beyoncé wanted 'to show the historical impact of slavery on Black love, and what it has done to the Black family', showcasing how Black women and men, torn apart by the violence of bondage and later battered with damaging stereotypes, were 'almost socialized not to be together'. When the film debuted on HBO on 23 April 2016, thousands speculated that *Lemonade*'s discussions of infidelity were autobiographical. They read the album as only a kiss-off aimed at Jay-Z. But, as has been mentioned, Beyoncé knew of her own father's previous affairs, and of the child he fathered with another woman while still married to Tina.

Patience, however, would repay those eager to know more. Almost two years after *Lemonade*'s release, Beyoncé spoke to American *Vogue* about the album's interpolation of legacy. 'I come from a lineage of broken male-female relationships, abuse of power, and mistrust,' she said. 'Only when I saw that clearly was I able to resolve those conflicts in my own relationship.' She also noted that she discovered one of her ancestors had been a white owner of enslaved people – she had to sit with that, to overcome what it meant. She added: 'I pray that I am able to break the generational curses in my family and that my children will have less complicated lives.'

Predictably, Beyoncé created a media storm by exploring the ugliness, depths and truths of the culture that shaped her. A day after releasing the 'Formation' video, she would perform the song during Coldplay's Super Bowl half-time show in, fittingly, New Orleans. Her backing dancers wore berets pinned over afros. Two ammunition bandoliers bearing gold bullets hung sash-like over Beyoncé's chest, as she stomped in heeled combat boots. Combined, the overall look evoked not only the Black Panther Party but also Michael Jackson's 1993 Super Bowl half-time show. The song makes lyrical nods to LGBTQ+ ballroom culture. And so that performance felt like a reinforcing acknowledgement for Black, queer and other marginalized people all over the world. And as such, it unsurprisingly inflamed anger and confusion in others. White America has rarely accepted militant Blackness, after all.

There is, ultimately, a certain duality to being seen as Black. White society often needs to assume a state of Black suffering, to rehash stories of slavery and an ongoing struggle for basic civil rights, in order to compute Blackness. But that is not its reality. To be 'Black' denotes a multitude of experiences, many proud and enriching. And yet a small, prominent sliver of those are often refracted through a lens created by white European ideas of race.

Blackness is thus perceived in opposition to whiteness: the evil to white innocence, the laziness to white productivity, the violence to white peacefulness and civility. These are all, of course, fabricated falsehoods. Being Black is not 'difficult', or painful, or a drain on one's mental health without the foil of whiteness. Eliminate racism and Black people will be freed of the double bind of being considered both 'other' and charity cases in need of 'saving'. With 'Formation', Beyoncé shattered the mirage of an apolitical existence. She also toyed with this very duality of pain and joy. The video placed both extremes flush against each other: a dancing Black boy facing a line of white police officers, for example, in one pivotal scene. She evoked a double meaning with 'in formation' – lining up, military-style, and seeking out knowledge.

But the imagery she deployed, of a cop car sinking in floodwater, was then read (and misread) as hostile by white Americans who still perceive Blackness as a source of violence and potential retribution. Rather than viewing her music video as a commentary, some saw it as an attack – which says more about white fragility than it does about Beyoncé. As she said herself, later in 2016: 'If celebrating my roots and culture during Black History Month made anyone uncomfortable, those feelings were there long before a video and long before me.' By this time, both Black Lives Matter in 2013 and then 2015's broader Movement for Black Lives had galvanized a new generation of Black activists. Beyoncé didn't make these creative and personal choices in a vacuum. She also knew that her work could be misinterpreted, just as the phrase 'Black lives matter' was so quickly twisted by white society to imply threat – 'only Black lives matter' – rather than understanding the statement as 'Black lives matter, too'.

She shared an open letter on her website in July 2016, addressing the killings of Philando Castile and Alton Sterling, demanding change and directing readers to activist sources. It was no secret that she and Jay-Z were willing to come out in defence of the families rocked by their loved ones' deaths during interactions with the police. Both had also publicly pledged their support for a gun control movement, along with other celebrities, in 2012. 'I'm an artist and I think the most powerful art is usually misunderstood,' she said in April 2016, to *Elle* magazine. 'But anyone who perceives my message as anti-police is completely mistaken.' She clarified her respect for the profession of policing before adding: 'But let's be clear: I am against police brutality and injustice.' That quote alone showed that Beyoncé would no longer sidestep tough issues. She faced them head-on.

* * * * *

Before April 2018, few people outside the US knew much about the tradition of homecoming at all, let alone its specific importance to historically Black colleges and universities (HBCUs). Beyoncé would change all that. Her performance at Coachella festival – postponed by a year – made her the first woman of colour to headline the event. More than that, it became a vessel through which to celebrate the institutions that had provided a hard-won education for her father, Maya Angelou, James Baldwin and countless other Black people – well-known or not. She honoured the annual, often week-long, homecoming in homage to them. It also, to be frank, nodded to a life she may have lived if she had had the time to attend university herself. The crux of her headline set rested on a clear purpose: sharing a part of the Black experience with a predominantly white audience at the festival itself, and then with an even larger audience when a corresponding concert film debuted on Netflix in April 2019.

Coachella – dubbed 'Beychella' by a bellowing DJ Khaled – allowed Beyoncé to honour the signifiers of the HBCU experience. The concert film punctuates interludes between the gig with behind-the-scenes, analogue-fuzzed scenes from rehearsals. Each builds towards a crescendo: Beyoncé's homecoming was designed to allow Black Americans to feel seen, on a global stage. They could essentially see layers to the Coachella set that others would have missed, like a secret language whispered across HBCU alumni networks and campuses. The thumping, driving brass band, the costumes, the meticulous step routines, the smile of baton-twirler Edidiong Emah – all were stitched together, a tapestry of Black specificity.

In 2020, Beyoncé returned to her Black ancestry as influence. In July, the sumptuous feature-length film *Black Is King* followed her *Lion King* companion album from 2019, *The Lion King: The Gift*. The movie reinterpreted the plot of the *Lion King*, sweeping across several countries on three continents to highlight the importance of family and being true to oneself. The album, however, wasn't a solo effort. Instead, Beyoncé handed the microphone to African and American artists and producers. She became, in essence, a curator. Turning the lens away from its usual position on herself, Beyoncé also pulled the stories of her dancers, backing vocalists and inspirations into her work. By returning to the site of her Blackness, she opened her arms to welcome those who could relate, too.

Where *Homecoming* zoomed in close on a particular set of rituals, *Black Is King* craned a neck, scanning over a pan-African, diasporic vision of pride. *The Gift* also felt like a sort of whistle-stop tour through the sonics and rhythms of South Africa, Nigeria, Ghana, Cameroon and Mali. Notably, East Africa does not prominently feature, even though the *Lion King* film was set in the Serengeti. Don't worry – East African fans have already made their disappointment known.

For both the album and film to feel authentic, rather than as though they were ogling at Africa from the outside, both projects needed direct connections to the continent. Beyoncé travelled to parts of Africa, certainly. A film about making *The Gift* (another piece of visual content to add to her growing library) flicks past street scenes in South Africa, Nigeria, Burundi, Egypt and Ethiopia. You see her children and husband along for the ride. But more than a slideshow of what could look like holiday snaps, she relinquished control, letting other artists take the lead from song to song. The list of singers, rappers and producers runs long but includes Shatta Wale from Ghana, Tiwa Savage, Bankulli and Burna Boy from Nigeria, Moonchild Sanelly and Busiswa from South Africa, as well as British singer-songwriters Labrinth and Raye. Atop this congregation, she casually sprinkled Kendrick Lamar, Tierra Whack, Pharrell and, of course, Jay-Z as hip-hop A-listers from the US. The album is credited to various artists. It is not, truly, a Beyoncé solo offering.

She didn't leverage those collaborations to cynically double down on the current trend of artists stuffing featured artists onto singles. There, the goal is to generate the most digital streams. Each voice here contributed to the chorus. Each perspective enriched Beyoncé's own and helped form the album's expansive and varied textures. They all, in their way, could make you whoop with joy or rotate your hips or sit still and reflect. The Blackness was the point.

As Beyoncé put it in 2019, 'I rarely felt represented in film, fashion, and other media. After having a child, I made it my mission to use my art to show the style, elegance and attraction in men and women of colour.' *Black Is King*, even more explicitly, went on to do this. Featuring African models and actors, it again saw Beyoncé take on more of a supporting role.

The film felt like a salve for many Black viewers, after a summer in which anti-Blackness became inescapable, thrust onto phone screens and news broadcasts. 2020 proved to be another year when Black people would be expected to watch a real-life snuff film – this time, displaying the death of George Floyd under a police officer's knee in May. Like Eric Garner before him (killed by police in New York in 2014), Floyd's final words, 'I can't breathe', became a protest mantra.

With *Black Is King*, Beyoncé once again tapped into that duality of pain and joy. She indirectly showed that where there may be trauma, in an eight-minute video of the life leaving a man's body, there could be righteous anger. There could be a call for change, the cathartic release of blasting a song loud, the quiet happiness of a baby cradled in her arms in the film's opening scenes. By openly advocating for Black people – including for twenty-six-year-old Breonna Taylor, a woman shot dead by police in her own home in March 2020 – Beyoncé could exhale.

XII.

Being the Greatest

Adele, star of blue-eyed soul, was eleven years old when she first heard Beyoncé's voice. A friend introduced her to 'No, No, No' by Destiny's Child. The moment, by her own admission, changed her forever. And so, aged twenty-eight, when she beat her idol to the 2016 Grammy for Album of the Year, she was in disbelief. She cried while accepting her award, heralding Beyoncé in her speech as 'the artist of my life'. That's the sort of admiration you're dealing with when you assess Beyoncé's impact. Almost every artist currently towering over the pop music industry has directly cited Beyoncé as an influence: Adele, Dua Lipa, Normani, Ariana Grande, Lady Gaga, Harry Styles, Sam Smith, Taylor Swift, Rihanna and even her peer Britney Spears. Outside music, academics have analysed and studied her work. Producer-actors Gwyneth Paltrow, Priyanka Chopra and Gabrielle Union, as well as gymnasts Gabby Douglas and Nia Dennis, and basketball player Kevin Garnett have all spoken about using her drive as a motivator. To list all the examples here would require far more pages than this book will allow.

What's particularly interesting is that her effect on other public figures and fans stems not only from her discography. Even if you're not a fan of Beyoncé's music, denying the ripple effects of her work ethic, artistic vision and social advocacy on millions of people globally is ultimately lying to yourself. She has become so famous, so successful, so respected by grasping onto the parts of herself that others see and buffing them to a reflective shine. Beyoncé shows others how to see themselves in what she does, makes and says. She hits a sweet spot of inspiration and awe repeatedly, making it her calling card.

As a child and teen, she witnessed the hidden machinery behind the music industry, clanging and hissing – burning many – and carrying artists along a conveyor belt. Some would fall off, losing relevance. Over the decades, this has never happened to Beyoncé. And that's because she applied those early lessons to each stage of her life from then on. By the end of her thirties, both her image and her purpose came into sharp relief.

Of course, there are commercial plaudits. Funnily enough, it would seem that a rundown of Beyoncé's sales would matter far less to her post-*4* than earlier in her career. But the stats are worth noting, purely to underline the scope of her appeal. Sweating fans scream themselves hoarse at her gigs, from São Paulo to Johannesburg to Tokyo, on account of how deep and far her music and image have permeated. *Dangerously in Love* remains her biggest seller, picking up more than 5 million US sales and an estimated 11 million global sales. From there, each of her albums on average sold about 4 million units in the US. She has earned millions from touring the world and sits atop an estimated US$420 million net worth.

Then: the awards. Beyoncé is the most-awarded artist at the MTV Video Music Awards, the BET Awards and the

Soul Train Awards. She has won definitive awards from the NAACP, GLAAD, Billboard, the George Foster Peabody Awards programme and the Council of Fashion Designers of America. As a solo artist, Beyoncé has won 24 Grammys – plus another four from her time in Destiny's Child. At the point of writing, she has been nominated 79 times, making her the most-nominated woman in Grammy history. As of 2021, she is also the most-awarded. She has not, however, won the most prestigious Grammy award, for either *Beyoncé* in 2013 or *Lemonade* in 2016. The Recording Academy still tends to categorize her as an R&B, rather than pop, artist. A racial dog-whistle sounds. In a rare awards press room appearance after the 2016 ceremony, Adele asked a roomful of journalists one question: 'What the fuck does she have to do to win Album of the Year?' Disgruntled fans would posit the same.

But as Beyoncé grew from sparky upstart to team leader, from sex symbol to a sort of unassailable force – someone granted deity-like status in breathless adulation – traditional signifiers of success started to matter less. After having Blue Ivy, her first child, her aims changed. 'Being "number one" was no longer my priority,' she said in 2019, reflecting on what felt like something clicking and changing inside of her. 'My true win is creating art and a legacy that will live far beyond me.'

And this, really, is what she has accomplished so far. Her music alone can light a fire somewhere in the pit of a listener's belly. Queer people and Black people tend to respond the most viscerally, hearing her call to them in *Lemonade* and *The Lion King: The Gift*. Straight men of varying ethnicities aren't impervious to her brand of empowerment either. Don't forget that she practised this skill from her teen years. Her songwriting laid out a blue-print with which to make women and girls feel strong. An anthem such as 'Survivor' could speak to so many people: those impacted by domestic abuse, divorcees, or simply someone commuting home after a gruelling double-shift at work. Over the years, she narrowed her focus from women to Black people and Black women. But her image and her sociopolitical statements still allow Beyoncé to make her art a site of universal connection.

If you look back to Beyoncé's cultural position around 2005, it would seem almost ridiculous to predict her trajec-tory. There's a hunger in her eyes in those early music videos; a precision to her live performances, all wind machine-blown hair and melismatic vocals. She was trying *so* hard – and every hour ended up being worth the strain. Over time, the world has watched her mellow and relax into being herself. She no longer sings at the top of her range, bending in fits of vocal acrobatics. No doubt, sitting back in her alto notes makes singing live while dancing easier. Now she even raps, a low, crackling and rhythmic rumble. All of those hours in the studio, from the time she was ten years old, have led to this point. She has far less to prove.

Family undoubtedly accounts for how Beyoncé's con-fidence has transformed over time. Her partnership with Jay-Z remains largely private. Nonetheless, it inspires endless shrill cries of 'couple goals!' and inspires a near-obsession with their joint earnings. They have collaborated for years, boosting each other up in the studio, onstage and away from prying eyes at home. *Beyoncé* directly referenced their sexual frisson. And yes, I'm aware that *Lemonade* seemed to growl at and chide her husband for alleged affairs. But she has always put those ideas into the music and never spoken about her marriage in any detail. Sitting on the *Oprah Winfrey Show* sofa in 2003, she plainly said it: 'I don't talk about who I'm dating or who I'm not.'

Blue Ivy's birth in 2012 forced Beyoncé to slow down, returning to music with the courage to upend the industry on her self-titled album. Having her twins in 2017 has also imbued her with a clearer view of what she will leave behind. As with so many of the billions of people who become parents, motherhood has sliced through her understanding of herself. Recurrent miscarriages hammered home what is at stake when you seek to replicate a part of yourself. She has spoken of being reborn as a result. 'I realized I had to take control of my work and my legacy because I wanted to be able to speak directly to my fans in an honest way,' she said in 2019. For this reason, she did away with the press as a conveyer of her stories. Her fixation on image-building has grown playful over time, captivating fans – whether on Instagram or in the myriad of films that now accompany and bolster her recorded music.

Ultimately, she has reframed control from looking like insecurity to being a source of quiet strength. She had to feel the sting of ceding that control, in her twenties, to understand its value. 'There were things in my career that I did because I didn't understand that I could say "no",' she has said. 'We all have more power than we realize.' That little girl, dancing on the deck in her back garden, became an icon. She discovered her power.

Resources

Discography

Destiny's Child
Destiny's Child, 1998
The Writing's on the Wall, 1999
Survivor, 2001
Destiny Fulfilled, 2004

Beyoncé
Dangerously in Love, 2003
B'Day, 2006
I Am... Sasha Fierce, 2008
4, 2011
Beyoncé, 2013
Lemonade, 2016
Homecoming: The Live Album, 2019
The Lion King: The Gift (Deluxe Edition), 2020

Further Reading

Books
Arenofsky, Janice, *Beyoncé Knowles: A Biography*, Greenwood
    Press for ABC-CLIO, 2009
Easlea, Daryl, *Crazy in Love: The Beyoncé Knowles Biography*,
    Omnibus Press, 2011
Kenyatta, Kelly, *Yes, Yes, Yes: The Unauthorized Biography*

of Destiny's Child – A Tale of Destiny, Fame and Fortune, Amber Books, 2000

Knowles, Beyoncé, Kelly Rowland and Michelle Williams with James Patrick Herman, *Soul Survivors: The Official Autobiography of Destiny's Child*, Pan Macmillan, 2002

Moore, Brian Kenneth, *The Making of a Child of Destiny: The Andretta Tillman Story*, Dousic Publishing, 2014

Pointer, Anna, *Beyoncé: Running the World: The Biography*, Hodder & Stoughton, 2014

Taraborrelli, J. Randy, *Becoming Beyoncé: The Untold Story*, Sidgwick & Jackson, 2015

Williamson, Joel, *New People: Miscegenation and Mulattoes in the United States*, The Free Press, 1980

Articles

Alvarez, Gabriel, 'Beyoncé: Mighty Fly', *Complex*, July 2011

Beyoncé, as told to Clover Hope, 'Beyoncé in her Own Words: Her Life, her Body, her Heritage', American *Vogue*, September 2018

Davis, F. James, 'Black Identity in the United States', in Peter Kivisto and Georganne Rundblad, eds, *Multiculturalism in the United States: Current Issues, Contemporary Voices*, Pine Forge Press, 2000

Dunn, Jancee, 'Date with Destiny', *Life, The Observer Magazine*, June 2001

Elberse, Anita, and Stacie Smith, 'Beyoncé', Harvard Business School Case 515-036, August 2014 (revised October 2014)

Enninful, Edward, "'I've Decided to Give Myself Permission

to Focus on my Joy": How Beyoncé Tackled 2020', British *Vogue*, December 2020

Good, Karen R., 'Taking Care of Business', *Vibe*, February 2000, vol. 8, no. 1

Hall, Michael, 'It's a Family Affair', *Texas Monthly*, April 2004

Hicklin, Aaron, 'Beyoncé Liberated', *Out*, April 2014

Newsome, Rachel, 'Destiny's Child Are Destined for Fame', *Dazed & Confused*, August 1999

Norment, Lynn, 'Destiny's Child: The Growing Pains of Fame', *Ebony*, September 2000, vol. LV, no. 11

Ogunnaike, Lola, 'Divas Live!', *Vibe*, February 2001

Okeowo, Alexis, 'Image Consultant', *The New Yorker*, 6 March 2017

Viewing

Beyoncé: Year of 4, 2011
Life Is But a Dream, HBO, 2013
Self-Titled, Parts 1 to 5, 2013
Yours and Mine, 2014
Lemonade, 2016
Girls Tyme – Making a Child of Destiny, Dousic Films & Television, 2017
The Lion King, 2019
Homecoming: A Film by Beyoncé, Netflix, 2019
Black Is King, 2020

Podcasts

Making Beyoncé, WBEZ Chicago, 2019
Dissect: Beyoncé – Lemonade, Spotify, 2020

Index

A

Aaliyah 19
Adele 117
Adidas 103
Aguilera, Christina 19, 41
Akon 67
Allure 74
Apple 92
Ashanti 58
Austin Powers in Goldmember
    57, 83

B

Backstreet Boys 19
Bailey, Chloe and Halle *see*
    Chloe x Halle
Bankulli 115
Bartlett, Liam 62, 65
Beck 97
Beem, Sophie 106
BET Awards 105–6, 118
BeyGood 63, 88, 105
BeyHive 67, 68–70, 80
Beyince, Angie 65
Beyoncé
    awards/nominations 44,
        50, 71, 97–8, 105–6,
        118–19
    'Baby Boy' 58, 59, 63
    B'Day 66, 91–2
    Beyoncé 89, 90, 91–4,
        97, 99
    Black Is King 109, 114,
        116
    childhood 5–6, 8–11,
        13–14; *see also* Girls
        Tyme
    'Crazy in Love' 52–3, 58,
        59, 66, 67
    'Dangerously in Love' 59
    Dangerously in Love 50–1,
        54, 58–9, 63, 97, 118
    'Deja Vu' 66
    'Drunk In Love' 98
    'elevator incident' 94–6

family 80, 86, 105, 110,
    119, 120–1
'Formation' 105, 109–10
4 75–6, 77, 78–9, 91–2
friendships 8–9, 14, 17–18,
    33, 42, 54–5
'Freakum Dress' 66
'Green Light' 66
Homecoming 113–14
I Am... Sasha Fierce 66–7
and Jay-Z, relationship with
    42, 52, 71, 78, 86
Lemonade 104–5, 108–12,
    119, 121
Lion King: The Gift 114–15,
    119
'Me, Myself & I' 59
'Naughty Girl' 59
'Pretty Hurts' 94
'Run the World (Girls)'
    78–9
and self-image 6, 43–4,
    47–9, 63–5, 80–6, 118,
    120, 121
'7/11' 87
'Sorry' 106
tours/touring 30, 60–1, 63,
    71, 72
'Why Don't You Love Me?'
    72
work ethic 14, 23–4, 48,
    51, 53–4, 71–2, 118
see also Destiny's Child
'Beyoncé Experience, The'
    63
Beyoncé World 68
BeyonceWorld.net 68
Billboard 40, 76, 79, 119
    charts 30, 38, 50, 58, 90
Björk 93
Black Eyed Peas 76
Black Lives Matter 112
Boyz II Men 30
Briggs, Kevin 'She'kspere'
    40–1

BRIT Awards 44
Burke, Ed 101
Burley, Ingrid 106
Burna Boy 115
Burruss, Kandi 40–1
Busiswa 115

C

Cadillac Records 76, 88,
    99, 104
Callahan-Longo, Lee Anne
    103–4
Carmen: A Hip Hopera 56–7,
    83
Carter, Blue Ivy 80, 86,
    119, 121
Carter, Rumi 105, 121
Carter, Sir 105, 121
Chi-Lites, The 66
Chicago Tribune 57–8
Chloe x Halle 106
Chopra, Priyanka 117
Coachella 43, 85, 113–14
Cody L 69
Columbia Records 102; *see
    also* Sony/Columbia
Council of Fashion Designers
    119

D

D'Angelo 93
D&D Management 15
Davis, Ashley Támar 18, 20,
    21–2, 23, 27, 34
Dazed & Confused 77
DeGeneres, Ellen 9
Dennis, Nia 117
Deréon, House of 60, 72,
    103
'Destiny Fulfilled...and Lovin'
    It' 60–1
Destiny's Child
    awards 44, 50
    'Bills, Bills, Bills' 38, 39, 40,
        41, 44, 46

Destiny's Child (contd.)
'Bootylicious' 42–4
'Bug a Boo' 39, 44
Destiny Fulfilled 60–1
Destiny's Child 30, 33–4, 35, 37, 44, 47
early years of 26–9
line-up changes/ disbanding 26, 30–3, 50, 54–5, 61, 95–6
'Hey Ladies' 37
'Independent Women Part 1' 39, 44
'Jumpin, Jumpin' 44
management of 16, 30, 31
and the media/ advertising 25–6, 31–2, 43–4, 48–9, 84, 95–6
'No, No, No' 117
'Say My Name 31, 33, 37, 55
'Survivor' 120
Survivor 44–5, 47, 56
tours/touring 30, 60–1
Writing's on the Wall, The 34, 37–8, 40–1, 44, 47
Douglas, Gabby 117
Drake 93
Dreamgirls 83

E
E! 84
Elektra Records 27–8
Elle 113
Eminem 93
En Vogue 15, 30

F
Facebook 85
Fela! 76
Felton, Pat 17
Fighting Temptations, The 57
Floyd, George 116
Frager, Arne 19, 21–2
Franklin, Aretha 41
Franklin, Farrah 31, 32, 33
Furtado, Nelly 67

G
Gaga, Lady 69, 117
Garnett, Kevin 117
George Foster Peabody Awards 119
Girls Tyme 5, 8, 14, 15–16, 17–24, 34, 45
'Talking 'Bout My Baby' 23
Glover, Donald 101
Gomez, Selena 69
Graham Norton Show, The 53
Grammys 50, 71, 97–8, 117, 119
Grande, Ariana 69, 117
Green, Philip 103
Guetta, David 76

H
Harris, Calvin 76
Harris, Tameka 'Tiny' 40
Harrison, Rich 66
Herman, James 16

I
I Am... (tour) 71, 72
Ienner, Don 55
Instagram 85, 86
iTunes 89, 90
Ivy Park 103–4

J
Jackson, Alonzo 'Lonnie' 5, 18–19, 21–2, 23, 28
Jackson, Janet 15–16
Jam, Jimmy 16
James, Etta 76
Jay-Z 42, 110, 112, 115
'Deja Vu' 66
'elevator incident' 94–6
marriage and family 71, 78, 86, 105, 120–1
'03 Bonnie & Clyde' 52
Jerkins, Rodney 37
Johnson-Bailey, Darlette 9–10

K
Kardashians, the 43
Kelis 41
King, Martin Luther, Jr 10

Knowles-Lawson, Célestine 'Tina' 7, 8, 10, 12–13
as role model 36, 45–7, 55, 83
stylist role played by 29, 45, 60, 63, 83
Knowles-Rowland Center for Youth, Houston 47
Knowles, Beyoncé Giselle *see* Beyoncé
Knowles, Mathew 7, 10, 36, 45–6
law-suits filed against 30–1, 32, 48, 58
managerial role played by 12, 16–17, 23, 48–9, 54, 77–8, 83–4
Knowles, Solange *see* Solange
Krausse, James 93
Kuti, Fela 76

L
Labrinth 115
Laday, Deborah 14–15, 16
Laday, Millicent 15, 18
Lamar, Kendrick 115
Latoisen, Staci 15
Lennon, John 10
Let's Move! 88
Lewis, Christi 15
Lewis, Terry 16
Life Is But a Dream 81, 87
Lion King 114, 115
Lipa, Dua 117
Live Nation 78
Locke, Lyndall 42
Luckett, LeToya
and Destiny's Child 25, 29, 30–1, 32, 48, 54, 95–6
and Girls Tyme 27

M
Making Beyoncé 21
Marshall, Terry 25–6
Matsoukas, Melina 110

Index

Met Gala, New York (2014)
94–5
Missy Elliott 37, 42
Monáe, Janelle 101
Moore, Brian 'Kenny' 17,
18, 21, 22
Moore, Mandy 41
Moore, Tony 'Mo' 21–2
Movement for Black Lives
112
MTV 31, 43, 71, 83
Carmen: A Hip Hopera
56–7, 83
Video Music Awards 72,
118
Mulligan, Mark 92
MySpace 82

N
Nava, Jake 52, 53
Netflix 113
New Edition 15–16
New York Times 58
Noel-Schure, Yvette 101
Normani 117
NWA 102

O
Obama, Barack 71–2
Obama, Michelle 71–2,
87–8
Obsessed 99, 104
Oprah Winfrey Show 73,
121

P
Paltrow, Gwyneth 117
Parkwood Entertainment
77, 78, 92, 99–101,
102–3, 104, 106–7
Phoenix House 88
Pink 41
Pink Panther 83
Pitbull 19
Plant Studios, Sausalito
21–2
Porter, Alisan 20
Porter, Billy 20
Powter, Daniel 67
Prince 102

Q
'Queen Bey' 94

R
Radiohead 93
Raye 115
Rihanna 69, 76, 117
Roberson, LaTavia
and Destiny's Child 25,
29, 30–1, 32, 38,
48, 54,
95–6
and Girls Tyme 15,
20, 23
Roc-A-Fella Records 42
Rolling Stone 40, 64
Rowland, Kelendria 'Kelly'
14, 17–18, 33, 54–5
and Destiny's Child 25,
29, 32, 43
solo career 50, 61

S
Sandra Rose 68
Sanelly, Moonchild 115
Sanneh, Kelefa 58
'Sasha Fierce' 11, 65–6,
73–4
Saturday Night Live 56,
69
Savage, Tiwa 115
Seals, Denise 14–15, 16
Simmons, Daryl 27–8, 37
Simone, Nina 41
Simpson, Jessica 41
Smith, Bessie 41, 102
Smith, Sam 117
Solange 8, 93, 95
Somethin' Fresh 24; *see
also* Girls Tyme
Sony/Columbia 29, 30, 35,
42, 58–9, 92
Soul Survivors... 16, 28,
56
Soul Train Awards 119
Spears, Britney 19, 41, 117
St. John's Downtown
United Methodist
Church, Houston
47
Star Search 18–20, 22–4
Style Savvy 72
Styles, Harry 117
Survivor Foundation 63
Swift, Taylor 72, 93, 117
SWV 15, 30

T
Taylor, Breonna 116
Taylor, Nikki 15, 21
Taylor, Nina 15, 20
Texas Monthly 64
That Grape Juice 68
Thomas, Lorenzo 39
Tidal 105
TikTok 87
Tillman, Andretta 16–17,
18, 22
Timbaland 37
Timberlake, Justin 19,
67
TLC 15–16, 30, 41, 102
'No Scrubs' 39–40, 41
TMZ 95
Topshop 103
Touré 64–5
Townsend, Robert 56
Tumblr 80, 81, 85–6
21 Savage 93
Twitter 68, 81
Tyler, The Creator 101

U
Union, Gabrielle 117
Usher 19

V
Vogue 96, 110
Voice, The 20

W
Wale, Shatta 115
Washington, Dinah 41
West, Kanye 72, 93
Whack, Tierra 115
Whites, Teresa LaBarbera
29, 93, 101
Wilbekin, Emil 84
Williams, Michelle 31, 33,
43, 50, 60
Williams, Pharrell 115
Wirtzer-Seawood, Lauren
87

Y
Yates, Reggie 82
Young, Jennifer 15

Z
Zekani, Sisa 67–8, 69–70

Acknowledgements

I'd like to thank Donald Dinwiddie, Robert Shore and the team at LKP for their support with the project. To my friends Steph Singer, Ashraf Ejjbair, Amy Herbert, Michelle Kambasha, Chiz Adizie, Katherine Mountain, Tom Mehrtens, Anna Mears, Victoria Parkey, Naomi Pallas, Sune Rasmussen, Harriet Gibsone and Ben Lee – thank you for gassing me up when I told you about the book and for being there when 2020 was doing a lot. Mum, Fifi, Gwilym, Dad – I love you. And of course to Beyoncé, for being Beyoncé.

Picture Credits
(numbered in order of appearance)

1. Tim Mosenfelder/Getty Images

2. Jeff Kravitz/FilmMagic, Inc./Getty Images

3. Frank Micelotta/Getty Images

4. David Surowiecki/Liaison/Getty Images

5. David McNew/Newsmakers/Getty Images

6. Kevin Mazur Archive 1/WireImage/Getty Images

7. Tsuni/USA/Alamy

8. Timothy A. Clary/AFP via Getty Images

9. Entertainment Pictures/Alamy

10. Bryan Bedder/Getty Images

11. Shutterstock/Featureflash Photo Agency

12. Shutterstock/arvzdix

13. Simon Bruty/Sports Illustrated via Getty Images

14. Gary Friedman/Los Angeles Times via Getty Images

15. Reuters/Alamy

16. Jason LaVeris/FilmMagic/Getty Images

17. Josh Brasted/WireImage/Getty Images

18. Noam Galai/MTV1617/Getty Images for MTV